Easy Composting

Created and designed by
the editorial staff of
ORTHO BOOKS

Project Editor
Cynthia Putnam

Manuscript Editor
Susan Lang

Writers
Jeff Ball
Robert Kourik

Photography Editor
Roberta Spieckerman

Designer
Gary Hespenheide

Ortho Books

Publisher
Richard E. Pile, Jr.

Editorial Director
Christine Jordan

Production Director
Ernie S. Tasaki

Managing Editors
Robert J. Beckstrom
Michael D. Smith
Sally W. Smith

System Manager
Linda M. Bouchard

Marketing Specialist
Daniel Stage

Sales Manager
Thomas J. Leahy

Distribution Specialist
Barbara F. Steadham

Technical Consultant
J. A. Crozier, Jr., Ph.D.

Address all inquiries to:
Ortho Books
Box 5006
San Ramon, CA 94583-0906

Copyright © 1992
Monsanto Company
All rights reserved under international and Pan-American copyright conventions.

5   6   7   8   9
94   95   96   97

ISBN 0-89721-243-6
Library of Congress Catalog Card Number 92-70583

THE SOLARIS GROUP
2527 Camino Ramon
San Ramon, CA 94583-0906

Acknowledgments

Editorial Coordinator
Cass Dempsey

Copyeditor
Toni Murray

Proofreader
Deborah Bruner

Indexer
Trisha Feuerstein

Layout by
Cynthia Putnam

Composition by
Laurie A. Steele

Associate Editor
Sara Shopkow

Production by
Studio 165

Separations by
Color Tech Corp.

Lithographed in the USA by
Webcrafters, Inc.

Special Thanks to
Michael D. Barclay
The Merchant family
Patricia Smith
Marcia Donahue
The Nadler family
Mary Wildavsky

Photo Assistant
Karen Heilman

Photographers
Names of photographers are followed by the page numbers on which their work appears. R=right, C=center, L=left, T=top, B=bottom.

Liz Ball: 16, 18, 40, 45T, 47, 49B, 51B, 78, 81, 83B, 84B, 87B, 88, 91
Karen Bussolini, Positive Images: 72B
David Cavagnaro: 6, 67T, 70
Thomas Eltzroth: 45B, 50, 82C, 83T
Derek Fell: 30b, 52, 53
Karen Heilman: 4–5, 17, 29, 68
Saxon Holt: Front cover, title page, 10–11, 26, 27, 31, 36–37, 43, 48, 49T, 54, 60–61, 63, 69, 74–75, 89, 90, 92, back cover BL & BR
Jerry Howard, Positive Images: 8, 28, 32, 34, 41T, 41B, 56, 80, back cover TR
Robert Kourik: 7T, 7B, 9, 51T, 58B, 71, 76, 77
Michael Landis: 14T
Elvin McDonald: 12, 30T, 38, 67B, 82T
Michael McKinley: 14B, 15, 20–21, 64, 72T
Charles Mann: 19, 23, 24, 46, 62, 65
Doug Menuez: 84T
Robin Pendergrast: 87T
Cynthia Woodyard: 22, 25, 33, back cover TL

Other Sources
Ashby House, Inc.; Glendale Heights, Ill.: 55
East Bay Municipal Utility District; Oakland, Calif.: 73
ECHO INC.; Lake Zurich, Ill.: 87T
Gardener's Supply Company; Burlington, Vt.: 58T, 82B, 85
Garden Way, Troy, N.Y.: 86
Jim Hanson Landscape; Martinez, Calif.: 10–11, 26, 43, 49T, 60–61, 69, 89, 92, back cover BR
The Natural Gardening Company; San Anselmo, Calif.: Front cover, title page, 4–5
Sequoya Nursery; Oakland, Calif.: 27, 31, 36–37, 48, 74–75, 90
Smith & Hawken; Mill Valley, Calif.: 84T, 89, 92, back cover BR
Really Special Plants and Gardens; Berkeley, Calif.: 27, 31, 36–37, 48, 74–75, 90

Front Cover
The garden waste in this wood compost bin will soon be transformed into a rich, humusy soil amendment.

Back Cover
Top left: This compost bin is within handy reach of the vegetable garden but well away from the house.

Top right: Organic waste is emptied regularly into the compost pile.

Bottom left: Finished compost is removed from the wire bin.

Bottom right: If the compost is too coarse, it can be sifted.

Title Page
This three-compartment compost bin fits discreetly into a raised-bed garden.

Easy Composting

Introducing Home Composting

With the help of this book, learn to convert yard and kitchen waste into a valuable soil amendment—and conserve scarce landfill space at the same time.

T he next best thing to the natural, earthy material blanketing the forest floor, homemade compost has long been valued by gardeners for its soil-enriching qualities. In fact, many experienced home gardeners consider a compost bin required equipment—just as necessary as a hoe or a trowel.

What these gardeners have always known is now becoming common knowledge because of the crisis in waste disposal. As landfill space decreases at an alarming rate, many state and local governments are looking to composting as a way of handling yard and kitchen waste. Consequently, in every region, homeowners are being encouraged to set up compost piles.

With a little time and effort, anyone can learn to make soil-enriching compost. The rewards are manifold. In addition to helping solve a critical problem, as a home composter you end up with a valuable product to improve your landscape. Backyard compost has the added merit of being virtually free, once a bin or other basic equipment is in place.

Other benefits aren't as easy to measure. The practice of composting brings with it enormous satisfaction: seeing your investment in time and labor result in a worthwhile product, enjoying the outdoors through the seasons, and returning something to the earth instead of just taking from it.

Regular use of compost made from organic waste found around the yard and kitchen fosters a healthy, lush garden.

Many schools have programs to teach youngsters about composting. These schoolchildren are preparing to spread finished compost around planting beds.

space and in developing alternate methods of dealing with waste. Everyone is being enlisted in the effort to accomplish these goals. Ordinary citizens are under pressure to recycle their yard waste, and municipalities are being forced to handle the waste produced locally at parks, golf courses, and other public areas.

About one third of the space in landfills is taken up by organic waste from yards and kitchens—just the type of material that can be turned into fertile garden compost. In a landfill, that waste may take decades to break down, because it's bulldozed under, compressed, and often subjected to contaminants. In a compost pile, the same waste may break down in months—or even weeks. Since composting offers a viable solution to a taxing problem, producing compost is obviously no longer a task just for gardeners. The dawn of the twenty-first century will probably see a full-scale yard-waste recycling effort in residential areas, and the hallmark of the effort will be a compost pile in every backyard.

Setting up your own compost pile produces many dividends. With a relatively small investment in time and money, you can contribute to the solution of a major problem. By processing the organic yard and kitchen materials instead of adding them to the ever-increasing trash stream, you help to reduce the pressure on scarce landfill space. At the same time, you enrich the soil and improve the health of the plants on your property. The beauty of vigorous, well-tended trees, shrubs, and flowers enhances the value of your home and is a source of pleasure to you and your neighbors.

In addition, people who have been composting for years invariably mention personal benefits that they derive from it. A deep sense of satisfaction and well-being flows from the physical activity involved in collecting the materials, building and turning a pile, and distributing the compost around the yard. Many home composters are also gratified to discover that participating in this elemental process brings them closer to the natural world in a fundamental, rewarding way.

However, until legislation in many states began to ban yard waste from landfills, nongardening homeowners had little incentive to learn about the benefits of composting—even though the practice is an ancient one, dating back thousands of years.

Composting has emerged as a topic of intense, widespread interest. In the past, discussions of the importance of compost and how to make it took place exclusively among gardeners, who have long recognized the value of this rich, dark, earthy material in improving the soil and creating a healthful environment for plants. Now, it's not unusual to overhear these conversations at the bank or grocery store, at service club meetings, among local government officials, and between neighbors. Suddenly, understanding how to make and use compost is in the public interest.

This newfound interest occurs as the problem of waste disposal climbs toward a crisis level. The public is keenly aware that landfills are brimming over and that very few new dumping sites are likely to open. As a result, there's broad interest in conserving landfill

Top: A compost pile can be freestanding and needn't be confined to a bin. Bottom: The tidy, well-organized composting area in the back of this garden features a wood bin as well as plastic garbage cans handy for storing raw materials or finished compost.

Early civilizations, including ancient Rome and Greece, practiced composting. Records show that farmers deliberately piled animal manure and soil or muck in such a way as to promote decomposition and then used the resulting product as fertilizer. Composting continued through the Dark Ages and the Renaissance. In the New World, both native Indian tribes and early settlers relied on composting to provide a nutrient source for their crops. The practice remained basically the same from its inception until the early twentieth century.

That's when Sir Albert Howard, a British colonist in India, invented the layering method of compost-pile construction. A scientist at the 300-acre farm of the Indore Institute of Plant Industry, Howard developed large-scale composting operations based on Indian and Chinese folk techniques. He devised a system in which layers of plant material alternated with layers of manure, in a ratio of at least three parts plant debris to one part manure. His ideal compost pile was freestanding and measured 5 feet high and 10 feet wide. In the early 1930s, Howard returned to England to educate his fellow Britons about composting. The Indore method soon became the standard by which experts built their compost heaps.

Howard and other early proponents of home composting praised the value of manure, any kind of manure, in the pile. Unfortunately,

A composting area doesn't have to be an eyesore. This compost bin is tucked out of sight behind a decorative rock wall.

the implication that manure is critical to successful compost has deterred many would-be home composters who have no ready access to manure. In fact, you can make excellent compost with just the organic waste found around your home.

Since Howard popularized composting, researchers have refined techniques and developed new products to make the process easier. Composting is firmly entrenched as part of the culture of serious gardeners—and now it promises to appeal to a larger public, thanks to its usefulness in waste disposal.

MODERN COMPOSTING OFFERS CHOICES

Perhaps the most important message of this book is that making compost need be only as laborious and time-consuming as you desire. If the thought of having to turn a pile every few days has put you off composting, you'll be glad to know you can make perfectly good compost by turning the pile only once or twice, or without turning it at all.

So many choices are available that developing an appropriate composting system isn't difficult. Just choose the method that suits the size of your yard, the time and energy you're willing to devote, and the amount of compost you can use. With a little planning, your compost pile won't be smelly or unsightly.

No matter what composting method you choose, you'll be amazed by the amount of material you can process. A single 3- by 3- by 3-foot compost bin can handle about a hundred bags of leaves, most of the weeds pulled during the season, grass clippings gathered occasionally, and some kitchen waste—all this in just one compost bin! By sitting in the bin, this organic waste is transformed into a valuable soil amendment for use around your shrubs or in a flower or vegetable bed.

Considering the enormous benefits of composting, there's every reason to join the legion of backyard composters. All the information you need to get started is in this book.

HOW THIS BOOK IS ORGANIZED

This is both an idea book and a how-to book. It's designed so you can browse through the pages and learn about the options for handling organic waste from your yard and kitchen. As you'll see, there's no one best way to manage waste or one best way to make compost. This book is organized to help you find the approach that suits your needs and to glean the information necessary to follow that approach. The major topics these chapters address include achieving zero waste management, understanding composting, making compost, using compost, and choosing composting equipment.

Achieving Zero Waste Management

If you produce only as much organic waste as you can handle in a compost bin, then composting alone will manage your waste load. But what if you produce more than you're able to compost? The second chapter offers ideas for reducing and reusing much of the waste generated by the average yard and kitchen. For example, you can drastically reduce waste by leaving grass clippings on the lawn—and if you don't want to do that, you can reuse them as mulch. You may be able to reduce and reuse so much organic waste that, at the composting stage, you have to deal with less than one quarter of the current volume.

Understanding Composting

Knowing how a compost pile works will be helpful as you establish and maintain your system. The third chapter examines the elements required to make a good pile, how the materials break down, and what you can do to control the process. Also included is information about the kinds of organic materials suitable for a compost pile, as well as ones that you should avoid.

Making Compost

The fourth chapter discusses the different approaches to making compost, from passive to highly managed compost piles, to sheet composting, to worm composting. The chapter includes detailed information on managing the composting materials so that you get good compost in the time desired. You will learn how to solve problems that may arise, as well as how to handle food waste without causing odors or attracting pests.

Using Compost

The fifth chapter expounds the myriad benefits of compost, such as improving soil structure and providing a nutrient reservoir for plants. Also, this section discusses the many ways to use compost, from working it into garden beds, to using it as a mulch, to making compost tea. If you can't produce enough compost, you can always stretch your supply by mixing it with other organic materials available locally. However compost is used, it will improve the soil and foster healthier, more productive plants.

Choosing Composting Equipment

There are as many different types of composting equipment as there are techniques for making compost. The sixth chapter helps you narrow the choices and reach a decision that makes sense for you—whether to build your own bin or buy a commercial one, what kind of bin to have, whether to obtain a shredder, and what additional tools and supplies will be useful.

Demonstration gardens where the public can learn about composting abound throughout the United States. Various types of composting devices are on display at this site in Seattle.

Aiming for Zero Waste Management

Here are ways to reduce, reuse, and recycle the organic waste from your yard and kitchen. You'll cut down significantly on trash and improve your yard at the same time.

Roughly one third of all waste dumped in overburdened landfills across the United States consists of garden clippings and kitchen waste—just the type of organic material most easily eliminated from the trash stream. By following the lead of the recycling movement, individual homeowners can reduce, reuse, and recycle this material instead of throwing it away. With planning, you can decrease the waste to zero, or nearly zero.

One of the most important ways to reduce yard waste is to leave grass clippings on the lawn to decompose. Instead of taking up valuable space in a dump, the clippings work their way into the ground, improving the soil and feeding the lawn. The primary way to reuse organic waste is to mulch with it. Mulching offers myriad benefits, such as protecting the soil, conserving moisture, and suppressing weeds. Recycling the waste through composting—the major topic of this book—is discussed at length in the ensuing chapters.

Even if composting is your primary interest, you'll find the ideas in this chapter helpful. Since yard waste isn't generated uniformly throughout the year, you may discover yourself with an excess of woody prunings in spring, a glut of grass clippings in summer, or a surfeit of leaves in fall. This imbalance creates a dilemma for anyone wishing to process waste solely through composting. This chapter offers options for dealing with each material.

A basic tenet of zero waste management is to reuse or recycle garden waste instead of throwing it into the trash. These clippings and pulled weeds will be added to the compost pile.

The volume of waste produced by American homes continues to increase at an alarming rate while the space available for dumping it rapidly diminishes. Most of us have developed an out-of-sight, out-of-mind attitude about trash, including the waste generated by yard care and meal preparation. Every year we set out millions of tons of organic materials at the curb, expecting municipal trash services to make it disappear. The arrangement has been an extremely convenient—and, until recently, a relatively inexpensive—solution to the waste problem.

Local and state governments are struggling to reduce the cost of managing landfills and to find alternative methods of handling trash. Organic waste from the home has been targeted by many governments, since it accounts for nearly one third of all waste dumped in landfills—and it's recyclable. This waste comprises three main categories: The largest volume consists of grass clippings; the next biggest is kitchen waste; the third largest component includes leaves, twigs, and other yard debris. Some states have prohibited the dumping of all or certain kinds of yard waste into public landfills, shifting the responsibility for processing the material to homeowners and to municipal and county governments. Many more states are expected to follow suit in the near future. It doesn't take much imagination to realize that in most parts of the United States over the next 10 years, homeowners are going to have to learn how to process much of their own yard and kitchen waste.

The big question is how far can individuals go in processing this waste? The answer is—much farther than they may have thought possible. More than 95 percent of yard and kitchen waste can be handled at home. Zero waste management is becoming a legitimate goal of the many community programs that have sprung up around the United States. With some knowledge, equipment, and time, it's a goal most homeowners can attain.

Of course, yard debris and food scraps aren't the only types of material thrown away in large volumes. The recycling movement adopted the motto *Reduce, reuse, and recycle* to encourage householders to limit the number of cans, bottles, and newspapers they contribute to the waste stream. The same motto applies to dealing with yard and kitchen waste.

Obviously, the volume of organic waste varies according to the size of a property and the types of plantings, but the model of reducing, reusing, and recycling is appropriate for any household. Most of the grass clippings currently collected and put out for trash pickup can be left on the lawn. This one action immediately reduces more than one third of the typical yard waste load. Reusing leaves as mulch eliminates nearly another third. The remaining third can be recycled through composting.

REDUCING WASTE

If your property contains an expanse of lawn and many trees, you may have more waste on your hands than you can reuse in the yard or recycle through composting. Here are some simple steps to reducing the volume of organic trash by as much as 50 percent—and you can do it without turning the lawn into a concrete patio or cutting down any trees.

Leave Grass Clippings on the Lawn

Why have most people developed the habit of collecting grass clippings instead of leaving them on the lawn? The answer is simply that almost all lawn mowers are equipped with bagging attachments. As a result, people have become accustomed to the sight of freshly mowed lawns devoid of clippings. They habitually bag the grass clippings because, until recently, municipal trash collection systems accepted them.

Leaving grass clippings on the lawn to decompose, a process called grass-cycling, offers many benefits. It improves the soil by restoring

A simple way to reduce the amount of yard waste is to leave grass clippings on the lawn to decompose. The clippings break down quickly, returning organic matter and nutrients to the soil.

Mulching Mowers

A mulching mower is designed to chop grass clippings into small pieces and distribute them evenly over the lawn, where they'll fall among the blades and work their way back to the soil. A conventional mower blows clippings out of a discharge chute, but on a mulching mower the chute is blocked off and a cutting blade shreds the clippings. For the best results, cut only about 1 inch of grass at once. Many models can do a good job of shredding tall grass, however.

Although mulching mowers were developed in the 1970s, they didn't come into their own until recently, when states began passing legislation restricting yard waste in landfills. Now more and more lawn mower companies are selling mulching models.

Consider getting a mower that converts from mulching to conventional cutting and bagging, since there may be times when you'll want to collect the clippings. For example, fall leaves can accumulate to such a thickness on the lawn that the mulching mower can't chop them sufficiently. You're better off bagging the combination of grass clippings and leaves for use as mulch or to add to your compost pile.

For more information about mulching mowers, see page 86.

Recommended Mowing Heights

Grass	Recommended Height of Mowed Lawn
Bahia grass	1½″–3″
Bent grass	¼″–½″
Bermuda grass	
Common	½″–1½″
Hybrid	½″–1″
Buffalo grass	2″–3″
Centipede grass	1″–2″
Fescue	
Chewing	1″–2″
Fine	1″–2″
Tall	2″–3″
Kentucky blue grass	1½″–2½″
Rye grass	1″–2½″
St. Augustine grass	1″–2½″
Zoysia grass	½″–1″

valuable organic matter, reduces the need for additional fertilizer, and saves you the time and labor currently spent collecting and disposing of the clippings.

Despite these benefits, many homeowners worry about the appearance of a lawn with clippings on it. However, since grass clippings consist of approximately 95 percent water, they break down quickly. If cut by a conventional mower, they usually dry out and decompose within a week or 10 days. They disappear in less than a week when they're cut with a mulching, or recycling, lawn mower (see Mulching Mowers above and on page 86).

Of course, clumps of clippings are unsightly and unhealthy, but an effective mulching mower prevents them. Even with a conventional mower, clumping won't be a problem if the correct lawn height is maintained. That means mowing often enough so you don't remove more than one third of the grass blade at a time. For example, to keep a lawn at 2 inches high, mow before it reaches 3 inches high.

To keep grass healthy, don't mow the lawn too short; see the chart above for recommended mowing heights of various lawn grasses. Grass maintained at the correct height keeps the soil cool, helps reduce water evaporation from the soil, and discourages annual weeds from germinating. More important, taller grass provides room for the clippings to fall into, thus helping prevent clumps on the lawn surface.

Many people resist leaving grass clippings on the lawn because they believe that the practice contributes to thatch—an impenetrable layer of grass roots and stems at the soil surface. Actually, chronic soil compaction, overuse of fertilizer, and improper watering are responsible for thatch. Unlike grass leaves, which are largely water, grass roots and stems are high in lignin, a fiber that breaks down slowly. When roots and stems crowd together at the soil surface and form thatch, they block the natural decomposition of grass clippings. Thatch problems are aggravated by allowing the grass to grow too long and then cutting it very short.

Decrease Lawn Size

Even if you don't leave grass clippings on the lawn, you can reduce the volume of clippings simply by reducing the size of the lawn. Most homeowners are living with the lawn configuration that was established by the builder or that was in place when they purchased the property. In the past, large lawns were the rule in many areas. Now, because of less time for yard care and diminishing landfills, replacing part of the lawn with a low-maintenance ground cover may be desirable. In arid regions, a limited water supply is another compelling reason to replace a section of lawn with a drought-resistant planting.

Grass is nothing more than an attractive ground cover that prevents the soil from eroding.

Top: A smaller lawn means less maintenance and fewer clippings to contend with. Bottom: Regular compost applications encourage healthy plant growth and reduce the need for supplemental fertilizer.

Many other ground covers can serve the same purpose and require less fertilizer, water, and maintenance than conventional lawn grasses.

Trees and shrubs grow better when the soil over their roots is covered with a mulch or ground cover rather than lawn. Grass competes with the larger plants for nutrients and water, and passing lawn mowers can seriously injure stems and trunks. Ground covers are especially useful for filling in areas where maneuvering a mower is difficult or where grass doesn't thrive, such as under dense shade trees.

Change Feeding Strategy

Excessive fertilizer stimulates growth that translates into extra clippings or prunings over the season. Plants are healthy more as a function of the health of the soil, rather than how much fertilizer is added each season. Reduce waste by adding only enough fertilizer to keep plants healthy. Since lawn clippings account for a major portion of the typical yard waste load, preventing overfertilizing of a lawn is particularly important. Several lawn-care measures can help make the most of what little fertilizer you do use. The most crucial is to leave grass clippings on the lawn to decompose. The organic matter provided by the clippings feeds the soil, which in turn feeds the grass. Aerate the lawn at least once each season to improve nutrient absorption from the soil.

Trees and large shrubs grow better when their roots are covered by a ground cover or mulch instead of grass.

Once this natural cycle of taking nutrients from the earth and then returning them is restored, the grass plants won't need as much supplemental fertilizer.

Change Watering Strategy

In areas where plants rely on irrigation water rather than rainfall, too much watering can cause excess growth that must be removed and disposed of. This is especially true of lawns—an overwatered lawn grows faster and needs more mowing than an adequately watered lawn.

The object of proper irrigation is to give plants only as much water as they need and only when they show signs of needing it. Stressing plants a bit is better than watering too soon. Don't rely on a dry soil surface to tell you when to water, since the surface always dries out before the root zone. Use a probe or stick to check whether the soil near the plant roots is still moist.

Learn to recognize when a plant needs water and let it go almost to that point before watering—don't go past that point or the plant may be damaged. Curling leaves are the first sign of water stress; the plant is reducing its surface area to cut down on water loss. Normally shiny leaves grow dull, and bright green leaves take on a blue or gray-green appearance. New growth wilts or droops; older foliage turns brown, dries up, and falls off. Flowers fade quickly and drop off early. Walking on a lawn can tell you if it's thirsty. If footprints remain after a few minutes, the lawn needs water.

In the West, many water companies are using a system based on the local evapotranspiration (ET) rate to help their customers figure out how much to water their lawns. *ET* refers to the amount of water that evaporates from the soil plus the amount transpired by the lawn. By knowing how much water was lost, you know how much to replace. Any additional water will only produce more growth, which means more clippings.

REUSING WASTE BY MULCHING

If you generate more grass clippings, leaves, woody prunings, and other organic materials than you're able to compost, then look for ways to reuse them. The easiest way to reuse yard waste is to distribute it as mulch—a protective layer of material spread on the soil surface.

Mulch offers many benefits. It conserves soil moisture so that plants can go longer between waterings. Mulch insulates the soil: In summer, it keeps the soil cool and prevents crusting; in winter, it shields plants from cold and helps prevent the cycle of freeze and thaw that kills many plants. Mulch helps protect the soil from erosion and keeps it from being compacted by foot traffic or heavy rains. A layer of mulch reduces runoff by slowing the flow of rain or irrigation water and letting it trickle into the soil. Mulch is invaluable for weed control: It keeps most weeds from sprouting, and those that do grow are easier to pull. Finally, as an organic mulch breaks down, it improves the soil.

Materials for Mulch

The best mulch is light and easy to spread but doesn't blow away readily or break down too quickly. It allows water to flow into the soil yet keeps soil moisture from escaping. It can be applied in a layer thick enough to inhibit weeds, without depriving the soil of oxygen. Every yard contains many organic materials—including some you may have been throwing in the trash—that meet these qualifications.

Surplus compost can be used as a mulch over tree roots. If your supply of compost is limited, use another mulching material, such as bark chips or chopped leaves.

Grass clippings   Although leaving grass clippings on the lawn is strongly recommended, there may be times when you want to collect

them and use them as mulch—for example, when you mow the grass after you have let it grow too long.

A mulch layer can be as thick as 4 inches, but be sure the clippings don't touch young plants. Before you use clippings as a thick mulch, you may want to let them dry first so they won't putrefy. Avoid pesticide-treated clippings, unless the grass received a thorough soaking after the pesticide was applied. If it hasn't rained, then wait until the next mowing to collect clippings for mulch.

Leaves   Chopped leaves make a much more effective mulch than whole leaves, which tend to mat. The easiest way to chop leaves is to run them through the lawn mower into a bagging attachment as you mow the lawn. That way, you mow the lawn and collect mulch at the same time. If your mower doesn't have a bagging attachment, control the pattern of mowing so that you're always blowing the leaves onto uncut grass. The leaves will go through the mower several times and end up well shredded in a pile in the center of the lawn. If you have a large volume of leaves, consider using a shredder.

Certain kinds of leaves contain substances that can be harmful to plants. These types include acacia, California bay, camphor, cypress, eucalyptus, madrone, oak, pine, pittosporum, red cedar, and walnut. Compost the leaves of these trees; don't use the foliage as mulch before the leaves decompose. In particular, always compost black walnut leaves. They contain juglone, which is highly toxic to many plants. Composting black walnut leaves breaks down juglone into harmless substances in 30 to 40 days.

Some researchers contend that maple leaves, which contain chemicals called phenols, have a harmful chemical effect on some plants. Experiments have shown that a maple leaf mulch around cole crops reduces the growth and yield by inhibiting root elongation. Early-season plantings are the most vulnerable because the phenols are released quickly when leaves that have been on the ground through the winter begin to decompose in spring. Fall crops aren't usually affected, since most of the phenols have leached by midseason.

Pine needles   An attractive mulch, pine needles have the advantage of decaying very slowly. You can rake them off a bed, store them in a pile, and use them later on another bed. They tend to acidify the soil, making them ideal around acid-loving plants, such as azalea, rhododendron, holly, viburnum, blueberry, and strawberry. You may not want to use them in areas of the garden where neutral or alkaline soil is desired. Pine needles help control several harmful soil fungi, including fusarium.

Shredded woody materials If you want to produce compost quickly, the best course of action is to limit the amount of woody material in the compost pile. Therefore, if your property contains many trees and shrubs, you'll probably want to reuse the majority of woody prunings as mulch or for paths (see page 19) rather than as a compost ingredient.

A 2-inch or thicker layer of shredded or chipped wood makes an excellent organic mulch that can take as long as two years to decompose. A chipper-shredder (see page 88) allows you to process woody trimmings quickly and efficiently.

Other mulching materials Although the materials listed previously are those most commonly used for mulching, you may have other equally effective materials available. Seaweed is a possibility if you live near the seashore and gathering seaweed that washes up on the beach is legal in your area. Rinsed first with fresh water, seaweed makes an excellent nutrient-rich mulch.

Papers, including newspapers, make an effective mulch. Because paper mulch isn't the most attractive, however, most people limit its use to the vegetable garden or other areas where the appearance of the mulch isn't important. Many gardeners shred the paper before applying it, but shredding isn't necessary.

Mulch Application

Although mulching isn't a complicated process, following a few guidelines can help you avoid problems.

Mulch thickness The most important guideline is not to make the layer too thick. Research has shown that a settled mulch more than 4 inches thick restricts the access of oxygen to the soil and to plant roots. Piled too high around a small tree or shrub, mulch can actually harm the plant over time.

An organic mulch such as chopped leaves settles quite a bit after it's spread. Start out with a 6- to 8-inch layer of leaves, because it'll settle to 2 to 4 inches within a month or so. Since wood chips don't settle much, start out with a 2- to 3-inch layer of that material. Spread mulch on soil that is moist but not soggy.

Timing Mulching fits into the seasonal garden cycle at specific times. When the leaves drop in fall, shred them and use them as a winter mulch on garden beds and around trees and shrubs. If other waste materials are also available at that time, use them for mulch too.

In early spring, remove the mulch from flower and vegetable beds so the soil can warm up. When the plants are established, lay the mulch again, leaving it in place until fall. Leave the mulch around trees and shrubs.

When a layer of mulch gets thinner than 2 inches, it doesn't suppress weeds well. If the layer becomes thin as the season progresses, add more mulch. In northern climates, two applications a year may be necessary to maintain the right coverage. In hot southern climates, where organic matter decomposes rapidly, three or four applications each year may be required.

By fall, the mulch should be partially decomposed, so work it into the soil during fall

Pine needles make an excellent, long-lasting mulch for acid-loving plants, such as impatiens.

A coarse mulch, such as large wood chips, tends to stay put on a slope.

cleanup to improve the soil. Then it's time to gather more mulching material and start the cycle again.

Problems With Mulch

Although mulching is an excellent way to re-use yard waste and benefit plants at the same time, some problems can occur unless you take precautions.

Cold soil   The soil beneath an organic mulch stays cold longer in spring than if the soil were bare. Remove all the winter mulch from flower and vegetable beds about three weeks before the last spring frost is expected. That will expose the soil to the sun, giving the beds time to warm up properly for spring planting.

Mulch instability   Keeping mulch on a hill-side or in a windy site is a matter of common sense and strategy. You'll quickly discover that a fine mulch tends to wash down a slope in a heavy rain, and a lightweight mulch is apt to blow away on a gusty day.

When laying a leaf or other lightweight mulch in an area exposed to wind and rain, hold the material in place with a scattering of coarse wood chips. Small branches and twigs

are also effective and look natural. As an alternative, lay down brush first, then add the leaves. The leaves will catch in the brush and stay put. Leaves that are kept moist are also more likely to remain in place.

Mice   Keep an organic mulch from touching the bark of a tree or shrub, since the mulch may harbor field mice during the winter. If the mulch is packed against the trunk, the mice will gnaw on the bark and seriously harm the plant. Avoid the problem by leaving about 2 inches between the bark and the organic mulch. In a cold-winter climate, you may want to remove mulch from around trees and shrubs temporarily in fall. After the ground freezes, restore the covering.

Slugs and snails   The bane of homeowners in many regions, these pesky mollusks feed at night and sleep under cool organic mulch during the day. The solution is not to get rid of the mulch, but rather to get rid of the pests. Initiate control measures early in the season, since slugs and snails are more difficult to eliminate once they're established. Consult a basic gardening guide or a pest-control book for information on controlling slugs and snails.

REUSING WASTE IN OTHER WAYS

Although mulching is probably the best way to reuse a significant portion of waste, other solutions may be applicable to your situation.

Wood Chip Paths and Driveways

If you have many trees and a heavy-duty chipper-shredder, you can turn brush and pruned branches into wood chips for paths or even a driveway. A 2- to 3-inch layer can eliminate problems with mud and keep away weeds. Wood chips also allow rain to soak into the ground instead of running off into the sewer, where it's wasted and may contribute to flooding problems.

Wood chips can be used for permanent paths in a raised-bed vegetable garden. They also make neat paths in heavily traveled areas of the lawn that have become dirt trails. In sufficient quantity, wood chips can even serve as a surface for a driveway or parking area.

Tree-trimming companies often give away truckloads of fresh shredded wood chips. Since home-shredded material is usually more attractive, lay the chips from the tree company as a base and cover them with your own chips.

Recycled Christmas Trees

More than 40 million Christmas trees are purchased each year in the United States. That means that municipal trash systems are burdened with up to 40 million dry, worthless trees every January. These trees can be put to good use in yards instead.

From January into spring, convert a Christmas tree into a bird-feeding station by hanging fruit, cones filled with peanut butter or suet, containers of birdseed, or bread crusts on the branches. Afterward, use a heavy-duty shredder to turn the tree, and those of your neighbors, into organic mulch.

An alternative is to remove the boughs and use them as mulch. Lay them on bulb beds and around acid-loving shrubs, such as rhododendron. Chop the trunk into fireplace logs.

Food Waste Fertilizer

Peelings, husks, leaves, and seeds from fruits and vegetables are loaded with nutrients that can be turned into instant fertilizer with the use of a sturdy blender or food processor. Pour

the liquefied kitchen waste around the bases of trees and shrubs or toward the back of garden beds, where it won't be visible.

Puréed fruit and vegetable waste decomposes quickly and disappears into the soil with no odor, and it doesn't attract pests. Within days, earthworms will pull whatever isn't fully liquefied into the soil, so the material virtually disappears in less than a week.

RECYCLING WASTE

The remaining yard and kitchen waste can be recycled through composting. The composting process strips the organic materials of their individual characteristics and transforms them into a rich, dark, humusy soil amendment that can be used throughout the landscape.

The chapters that follow discuss specific aspects of backyard composting. The third chapter explains how composting works; the fourth chapter gives instructions for making compost; the fifth chapter contains tips for using the finished product; and the sixth chapter discusses composting equipment and tools.

Reusing yard and kitchen waste as mulch or recycling it into compost are the goals of conservation-conscious gardeners. Applied generously around plantings and on pathways, these reclaimed waste materials promote a healthy, attractive landscape.

Understanding Composting

A basic grasp of the decomposition process is essential for anyone who wants to master the art of backyard composting.

Y ou're more likely to be successful as a home composter if you know something about the way a compost pile works. What's involved in the decomposition of organic matter? Should a pile be a certain size? Should certain kinds of organic materials be included? Why does one pile decay swiftly and another break down over a period of years? This chapter delves into these and many other major issues.

As you'll discover, compost is the end product of a complex feeding pattern involving hundreds of different organisms, including bacteria, fungi, worms, and insects. What remains after these organisms break down organic materials is the rich, earthy substance that gardeners value so highly as a soil amendment. The more efficiently these creatures feed, the faster they produce compost. In this chapter, you'll learn about the conditions under which the organisms flourish. You'll be able to apply this practical knowledge when you build your compost pile. In fact, the quality of your pile and the speed with which it decays will depend on how fully you provide the ideal conditions.

This chapter also includes information about the many kinds of organic materials suitable for a compost pile, as well as ones that you should avoid.

Backyard composting reproduces on a small scale the decomposition of organic materials that occurs naturally on a forest floor.

HOW COMPOSTING WORKS

Backyard composting replicates the natural system of breaking down organic materials on a forest floor. In nature, organic debris such as leaves, cones, twigs, berries, and even entire fallen trees eventually decompose to become a rich, dark material that resembles the black potting soils sold in garden centers. This decomposition process is essentially the same whether it takes place in the woods or in a backyard compost bin.

Compost is the result of the activity of billions of tiny organisms that utilize the two main chemical components of organic matter—carbon and nitrogen—in their life processes. They consume the carbon for energy and the nitrogen for growth and reproduction. The portion they can't digest remains as humus, or partially decomposed organic matter.

The interrelated feeding patterns of the organisms in a compost pile fuel the composting process. The by-products resulting from the digestion of one type of organism become the food source for another type of organism. The organic material undergoes progressive decomposition as it moves through the food chain. Eventually, most of the digestible material is consumed and transformed, leaving the dark brown or black humusy substance known as compost.

By providing the right environment for these organisms in your compost pile, you'll produce excellent compost. The decomposition rate is directly proportional to the numbers of organisms present. Once decomposition begins, it proceeds more rapidly as the microbe populations burgeon and greater numbers of organisms are available to break down the organic matter. Without the right conditions, you'll still get compost, but it may take a long time or you may encounter some undesirable side effects, such as unpleasant odors.

Organisms in a compost heap need a proper ratio of carbon-rich and nitrogen-rich materials. Carbon materials, which are dry or brown, include dried leaves, straw, and wood chips. Nitrogen materials, which are fresh or green, include grass clippings, animal manure, and kitchen scraps. Also the organisms need air and sufficient, but not too much, moisture. These four elements—carbon, nitrogen, air, and water—in approximately the right proportions are essential to the success of your composting operation.

Although any compost pile containing some of each element will decompose in time, controlling the variables allows you to increase the efficiency of your operation. Awareness of these factors can also help you prevent problems with the pile.

Prunings and pulled plants from this vegetable garden are added regularly to the compost bin. Given the right conditions, tiny organisms feed on the waste, transforming it into the dark, earthy substance called compost.

Proper Materials

Almost any organic material, alone or in combination with other organic materials, is appropriate in a compost pile. (See pages 28 to 35 for lists of commonly used materials; a list of unsuitable materials appears on page 35.) Mixing certain types of materials or changing the proportions can make a difference in the rate of decomposition. Leaves alone will decompose, but leaves mixed with grass clippings and kitchen scraps will decompose faster and more thoroughly. Although kitchen waste by itself will decompose, it will probably smell bad and may attract pests. Mixed with leaves or straw, it will decompose quickly and without any offensive odors.

You need to know how to achieve approximately the right mix of carbon and nitrogen materials so the composting organisms have a healthy balanced environment. See Proper Mix, which follows, for information on doing this. The more efficiently the organisms can feed and reproduce, the faster the pile will decompose—and it will do so without smelling bad.

Proper Mix

A balance of organic materials, some with a high carbon content and others with a high nitrogen content, is the ideal composting recipe. In the past, composting practitioners often expressed this ratio as a scientific formula. Now, many experts feel that, for the home composter, achieving the proper mix is more an art gained through experience than an exact science.

To succeed, you need a general understanding of the carbon-nitrogen ratio of a compost pile—in other words, of the proportion by weight of carbon to the proportion by weight of nitrogen in the pile. According to scientists, the ideal ratio of raw materials is between 25 and 30 parts carbon to 1 part nitrogen by weight. When the pile has decomposed, the ratio is about 15 to 1. That's close to the ratio of carbon and nitrogen in good garden loam or humus from the forest floor.

The challenge for a home composter is to learn how to achieve this ratio without having to worry about the numbers. The simplest method is to use roughly equal volumes of carbon and nitrogen materials—doing so should produce good compost. With a little experience you won't be conscious of measurements; you'll be able to estimate when you have roughly the right amounts of each type of material.

You need only to understand in approximate terms how the ratio affects a pile so you can make adjustments as necessary. For example, too much carbon (a ratio of more than 100 to 1) causes a pile to decompose very slowly. The reason is that it takes time for the organisms to generate a population large enough to consume all the carbon in the pile. The solution is to add more nitrogen-rich material.

Proper Particle Size

The organisms that break down organic material need oxygen to live and reproduce. Therefore, they feed on surfaces that are in contact with the air. The smaller the pieces of organic material are, the more surface area is exposed to the air and the faster the organisms decompose them.

A rich nitrogen source, such as fresh food waste, is needed to balance the carbon content of a compost pile. Without enough nitrogen, a pile decomposes slowly and fails to heat up.

An easy way to aerate a small pile in a wire bin is to lift up the bin and set it in a new location and then shovel the materials back inside.

Chopped, shredded, split, or even bruised organic materials always decompose faster than whole ones. For example, chopped leaves break down in less than one year, whereas the same volume of whole leaves takes nearly two years to decay.

Proper Volume

Organic materials, such as leaves, decompose whether they're spread in a relatively thin layer on the forest floor, heaped into a pile, or stuffed into an enclosure. However, the rate of decomposition is faster and more thorough when the materials are piled rather than spread thinly. By mounding organic material you increase its mass and generate larger populations of organisms. That's why it's advisable to build a pile of some sort—either a freestanding pile or one in a container or enclosure.

The size of the pile is only important if you want to produce high temperatures inside the pile. The minimum volume for effective decomposition at high temperatures is approximately

3 by 3 by 3 feet. A smaller pile doesn't have the critical mass to generate the amount of microbial activity necessary to efficiently decompose the material in high heat. The upper limit for a home compost pile is approximately 5 by 5 by 5 feet. A larger pile has reduced air access in the middle of the pile, which significantly slows the decomposition process and lowers the internal temperatures.

Proper Air

Effective decomposition requires plenty of air. Organic materials can decompose without air— that is, under anaerobic conditions—but the process is quite slow. One of the benefits of building a pile from organic materials that vary in size, texture, and coarseness is that the pile is filled with air pockets.

Turning the pile speeds the composting process by introducing air and stimulating microbial activity. If you never turn the pile and don't find some other way to aerate it, then the air is slowly used up; bacteria that function in

The microorganisms that break down organic materials are found naturally on plant parts and other waste in a compost pile. Since the organisms are also abundant in healthy soil, many home composters throw a handful of soil on the pile for insurance.

little or no air take over the decomposition process. Although the pile continues to decay, the process takes much longer. See page 48 for ways to add air to a compost pile.

Proper Moisture

Water is essential to the composting process, but it must be present in the right amount. Too little water causes decomposition to slow down. Too much water floods the air spaces, forcing air out of the pile and causing it to become smelly.

A well-maintained compost pile consists of 40 to 60 percent moisture. Such a level is similar to that of a sponge that has been soaked and then wrung out so it's just damp. Test your pile by picking up a handful of compost material and squeezing it tightly in your hand. If water drips out, the pile is too moist. If the material feels dry, it needs water. See page 50 for information on managing moisture.

Proper Organisms

Although all the variables mentioned previously are important, no decomposition takes place without the organisms that do the actual work of breaking down the pile. The microorganisms, which break down materials chemically, include several types of bacteria, fungi, and actinomycetes. The larger invertebrates, which break down materials physically, include

earthworms, centipedes, mites, nematodes, pseudoscorpions, rove beetles, sowbugs, springtails, and symphylans.

Bacteria These microscopic organisms play the biggest role in digesting the materials in a compost pile. The surfaces of organic materials contain many types of bacteria, most of which are dormant until the proper conditions allow them to begin multiplying and fulfilling their role in the decomposition process. Three main types of bacteria—psychrophiles, mesophiles, and thermophiles—are involved, each performing best in a specific temperature range.

Psychrophiles do most of the wintertime work, since they prefer cool temperatures as low as 28° F. Although materials don't decompose at temperatures below that level, the middle of a compost pile is usually that warm even during weather below 28°F. As the psychrophiles digest carbon in the organic materials, they generate heat.

When the temperature in the pile reaches 60° to 70° F, the mesophiles take over. If you start a compost pile in the middle of summer, the mesophiles may start the process, bypassing the psychrophiles. Responsible for most of the decomposition in a home compost pile, the mesophiles are active up to 100° F. Getting a pile to heat up beyond that temperature isn't

A well-built pile containing a suitable mixture of carbon and nitrogen materials heats up rapidly, producing steam when the materials are turned.

necessary unless you need to generate higher temperatures to kill disease organisms and weed seeds.

Under optimum conditions, the mesophiles work so hard at digesting carbon that they raise the temperature above 100° F and are replaced by the thermophiles. These are the bacteria that raise the temperature high enough to kill pathogens and weed seeds. Although 131° to 140° F is the optimum temperature range for compost produced under high temperatures, the thermophilic bacteria can raise the temperature even higher. However, if you allow the pile to get too hot—above 160° F—you risk killing the beneficial organisms, including the thermophiles, and ending up with sterile compost. If necessary, cool the pile by turning it.

When the thermophiles have finished their job and the pile cools down, the mesophiles take over again and decompose the remaining material.

Fungi   Although these microorganisms play a smaller role than bacteria, they're vital to the decomposition process. They break down cellulose and lignin, the resistant fibrous and woody parts of the organic materials, after the faster-acting bacteria make initial inroads on them.

Actinomycetes   A transitional group between bacteria and fungi, these microorganisms

break down organic matter in the later stages of decomposition. They reduce lignin and other resistant materials, and they secrete digestive enzymes that help decompose cellulose, protein, and starch.

Larger invertebrates   The various insects, mites, and worms that inhabit a compost pile contribute to the decomposition process in several ways. As they feed on the raw materials in the pile, they break them into smaller pieces, making them easier for microorganisms to process. As the larger invertebrates wiggle around and burrow in the pile, they transport the tiny microorganisms from one site to another, helping to distribute them throughout the heap. Finally, after these larger residents of the compost pile digest organic material, they excrete it. Their castings represent the decomposition that has taken place within their bodies.

When rising temperatures make the interior of the compost pile too hot to tolerate, the larger invertebrates migrate to the outer, cooler parts of the pile, returning when the microbial activity subsides and the temperature drops.

At various stages in the complex food chain within a compost pile, certain invertebrates feed on microorganisms as well as on other invertebrates. For instance, mites and springtails eat fungi, and nematodes eat bacteria. The mites, springtails, and nematodes, in turn, are preyed upon by pseudoscorpions, which are eaten by other invertebrates. Each type of organism becomes food for an organism higher on the food chain. At the end of the chain, beetles, millipedes, sowbugs, slugs, and snails ingest plant tissue, the raw materials in the pile.

THE DECOMPOSITION PROCESS

The natural decomposition of organic materials takes place in three steps: degradation, conversion, and curing. The materials in a compost pile will go through these steps whether you ignore the pile for a year or turn it every few days.

During the degradation phase, the organic materials are broken down. At its simplest level, the phase involves microorganisms consuming proteins and carbohydrates in the materials. As the microorganisms feed and multiply, they create energy in the form of heat and release water and carbon dioxide. Then these microorganisms become dormant or are consumed by other microorganisms, whose populations are burgeoning. The temperature in the pile rises.

It is during the conversion phase that humus—a rich, dark, earthy substance—is built. The temperature of the pile drops, and microorganisms that work at lower temperatures take over and complete the decomposition. At this stage, the compost is considered to be fresh, or raw. It can be used now, although it will continue to decompose. When fresh compost is dug into the soil, the organisms that break it down further will consume some of the soil nitrogen, depriving plants of it. For that reason, fresh compost isn't considered as valuable as compost that has cured.

During the curing process, microbial activity subsides; the pile cools down; and earthworms, insects, and mites gradually return. As the compost sits, it continues to decay. When you have a brown or black substance that looks and smells like humusy soil, you can assume your compost is mature. After it has cured even longer, the compost is considered aged. Beware of letting compost cure for too long—the longer it sits, the more nitrogen it loses.

The length of time compost takes to cure depends on the raw materials used to build the pile. A compost made from chopped leaves and chicken manure will probably become mature in seven or eight months and aged in about two years. A garden compost made exclusively from plant materials may cure twice as fast.

THE FINAL PRODUCT

After the chemical and physical breakdown of organic material is complete, what remains is compost. You'll notice that the pile of composted material is one-half to one-quarter the size of the pile you started with. The final product consists largely of microbial cells and skeletons; partially decomposed particles of fibrous and woody organic matter; and inorganic particles, including glass, sand, rock, and other mineral elements. The composition of compost varies from pile to pile. The makeup of the final product depends on the raw materials from which the compost is made, and no two home compost piles are likely to be exactly the same.

The average home composter won't be able to manage the composting process well enough to have any control over the nutrient content of the final product. Compost from different piles will contain varying amounts of nitrogen, phosphorus, potassium, calcium, and other nutrients. Having precise percentages of each nutrient isn't as important as having an ample supply of compost. Regardless of its chemical makeup, compost is an outstanding soil amendment.

The nitrogen content of a particular batch of compost is a function of the amount of nitrogen in the ingredients and the composting method used. Knowing with accuracy the amount of nitrogen contained in materials gathered from the yard and kitchen is difficult. Compost produced under high temperatures tends to have a somewhat higher nitrogen content than that produced under lower temperatures.

You can add rock powders to the pile to manipulate the phosphorus and potassium content of your compost. Adding limestone to a pile influences the amount of calcium in the final product, although a dose of limestone causes a loss of nitrogen, also. (For more information, see Adding Amendments on page 45.)

Compost is ready to use when the organic waste has decayed into a relatively homogeneous material that looks and smells like humusy soil. Sifting homemade compost yields a fine-grained product similar to commercially produced compost.

Many home composters are concerned about the pH—the relative acidity or alkalinity—of their compost. Most homemade compost produced from yard waste has a pH of between pH 6.8 and 7.2, which is close to neutral. Scientists disagree considerably about how the pH of the raw materials relates to the pH of the final product. Some reports indicate that compost made exclusively from acidic oak leaves has an acidic pH after decomposition is complete. In other experiments, the same ingredients produce a neutral compost. Experts can't even agree on the reason some composts are acidic and others alkaline.

If you use a variety of materials to make compost, you probably don't have to worry about the pH of the final product. If your plants are doing well, then compost produced from the prunings or leaves from those plants should be suitable for amending the soil.

Test the pH of your compost if you suspect a problem. Home soil-testing kits give approximate but useful pH readings. A soil-testing laboratory can perform a more accurate test and provide recommendations to correct any problems. In most cases, you should adjust the pH only if the compost is extremely acidic or extremely alkaline.

MATERIALS AT HAND FOR THE COMPOST PILE

Compost can be made from almost any kind of organic material, although most backyard composting systems use yard debris and kitchen scraps. This section describes common composting materials found around the home.

Leaves

For homeowners with deciduous trees, leaves represent a large percentage of total yard waste.

In many areas of the United States, fallen leaves constitute the major source of carbon for the compost pile.

Use the majority of the dried leaves for mulching. The remaining supply makes an excellent carbon-rich material for the compost pile.

Any kind of leaves can be composted. Even tough or waxy leaves can be added to the pile, although they take longer to decompose. You may not want to use the leaves of very weedy plants, such as Algerian ivy, if they're attached to persistent stems or root fragments that may survive composting. Most leaves containing substances that are toxic to plants lose their toxic effect through composting. For example, black walnut leaves are no longer a problem after they have been composted for 30 to 40 days.

Whether the leaves you use are naturally acidic or alkaline, composting tends to neutralize their pH. The resulting compost can be used anywhere in the landscape.

Pine Needles

An excellent material for mulching acid-loving plants, pine needles can also be composted. As with other acidic foliage, composting tends to neutralize pH. Pine needles take longer than most leaves to decompose fully, since they're covered with a thick waxy coating. Shredding the needles helps speed decomposition.

Grass Clippings

As discussed in the second chapter, the best course is usually to leave clippings on the lawn, where they can feed and revitalize the grass. In some situations, however, putting grass clippings into the compost pile is expedient, but you should mix them with a carbon-rich material, such as dried leaves, straw, hay, sawdust, or shredded paper. If grass clippings alone are piled into a compost bin, the pile quickly becomes anaerobic, or devoid of air, and starts to smell.

If you have access to large amounts of grass clippings for composting, dry them before adding them to the heap. Spread the freshly cut grass on a driveway or other paved surface to bake in the sun for at least a day. Once the grass dries and begins to turn pale and straw-like, it can be put in a compost pile without danger of putrefaction.

It's best not to compost grass clippings that contain pesticide residue. If a steady rain washes the grass after pesticide application and before mowing, the clippings can be composted, because the rain has washed the residue from

the blades down into the soil. If there is no rain, then wait until a later mowing to collect clippings for the compost pile.

Sod

Occasionally, a landscaping project or lawn renovation requires the removal of sod from lawn areas. Although sod makes effective compost, it requires a year or two to become fully decomposed. You can accelerate the process by running the sod through a heavy-duty shredder and mixing the pieces with carbon-rich material in a compost pile. Shake off loose soil before shredding the sod.

A slower method of composting sod is to dampen the pieces and stack them, grass side down. Throw a tarp or other covering over the sod to keep out light. The pile will be mostly compost after about two years.

Weeds

With a few exceptions, annual and perennial weeds compost easily. Treat them like grass clippings: Either dry weeds before composting

Pine needles left where they fall make an attractive, natural mulch. However, the needles can be composted if a surplus accumulates or if the compost pile is short of carbon-rich materials.

Top: These herbaceous prunings and pulled flowers are headed for the compost bin. Bottom: Woody waste is forked into a wire holding bin as part of fall cleanup.

them or mix them with plenty of carbon-rich material if they're fresh. Large amounts of freshly pulled green weeds represent an over-load of nitrogen-rich material that can settle into a tightly packed, bad-smelling mess.

Most weeds and weed seeds are killed when the pile achieves an internal temperature of 131° F, but some may survive. To avoid prob-lems don't compost weeds with persistent root systems and weeds that are going to seed. Also avoid weeds with sharp thorns and weeds that may cause an allergic reaction, such as poison ivy or poison oak.

Woody Materials

Even when wood chips, pinecones, cleared brush, and other woody materials are shred-ded, they take a long time to decompose. A heavy-duty shredder can cut up small branches into particles fine enough to be added in lim-ited amounts to a compost pile. However, if you have a large amount of woody material, use most of it as mulch or compost it separately so it can rot completely without slowing decompo-sition in the regular compost pile. Finished compost made from woody material may have a slightly coarse texture, but it's fine for use in all situations.

Some composting references suggest inter-spersing small branches and brush among the other materials in a compost pile to allow air to

Be stinting when adding wood ash to a compost pile. Too much can make the finished compost more alkaline than desired.

get into the center of the pile. The branches actually hinder more than help, since they must be sorted out of the final product. There are better ways to get air into the pile (see Managing Air on page 48).

Avoid composting scraps of pressure-treated lumber. Some trees—such as black walnut, eucalyptus, and red cedar—produce chemicals that can, in the wood, survive composting and inhibit plant growth in areas where the finished compost is used. Many of the tree species that can chemically impede other plants contain strong aromatic oils; you may want to avoid putting such wood in the compost pile. Instead, consider chipping the wood of aromatic trees and using the chips for permanent pathways or driveways. If you decide to compost the wood, do so with caution and be on the lookout for any problems.

Wood Ashes

Ashes from a wood-burning stove or fireplace—but not from a coal stove, charcoal barbecue, or other source—can be added to the compost pile. Do so sparingly, however, since ashes are alkaline. To a standard-sized pile (a cube measuring between 3 and 5 feet on each side), add no more than two gallon-sized pailfuls. Ashes are most useful when you're composting acidic materials, such as pine needles or oak leaves, because they'll move the compost

toward alkalinity. Although ashes add potassium and phosphorus to compost, they also cause some loss of nitrogen.

Paper

Much of the paper generated by households can be composted. Since newspapers are now printed with water-based inks, newspaper compost can be used even in the vegetable garden. Magazines printed in color on glossy paper are more problematical. Don't reuse them as mulch or include them in a compost pile. The paper used by computer printers or photocopy machines is also suitable for composting.

The secret to composting paper is to shred it first. The ideal tool is a paper shredder used in offices. A landscape shredder can work too, but use it on a calm day or bits of paper may be blown all over the neighborhood.

The best use for shredded paper is not as material in a compost pile, but rather as bedding in a worm box. See page 57 for more information on this type of composting.

Kitchen Waste

The average household produces more than 200 pounds of kitchen waste every year. If you take the managed approach to composting (see page 39), you can successfully compost all forms of kitchen waste. However, meat, meat products (including juices, grease, gravy, and bones),

If the yard and kitchen don't provide enough raw materials for the compost pile, look for an outside source. This load of apple pulp from a cider plant is earmarked for home composting.

dairy products, and high-fat foods (including salad dressings, mayonnaise, and peanut butter) present problems if they're put in a passive compost pile (see page 38). Exclude these items unless you take precautions (see Handling Food Waste on page 44). Although meat scraps and the rest will decompose eventually, they can smell bad in the process and may attract pests.

Vegetable and fruit peelings and other non-meat leftovers, even eggshells, can go into any compost pile. So can common garbage items, such as coffee grounds, tea bags, and used paper napkins. To keep kitchen waste from smelling, mix it with a dry carbon-rich material, soil, or old compost.

Composting systems designed to handle kitchen waste without causing odors or pest problems include worm boxes, compost tumblers, and kitchen waste digesters. (See page 57 for discussion of worm boxes; page 54 for compost tumblers; and page 85 for kitchen waste digesters.)

Human Waste

Do not add human feces to a compost pile. If it's important to you to recycle this organic material, then purchase a waterless, or composting, toilet. Models range from large units that rely solely on the natural processes of decomposition to smaller ones aided by electricity. A composting toilet collects human as well as kitchen waste and composts it inside the device. The final product is a rich compost that can be used throughout the landscape, although placing it near food crops is not recommended.

Human urine is a candidate for the home compost pile. Urine from a healthy person is sterile and contains no pathogens that can be transmitted to others. Very high in nitrogen, it can be used to accelerate the decomposition process in a compost pile that consists mostly of carbon-rich materials. Use it full strength, or dilute it as much as 5 parts water to 1 part urine. To prevent odor, sprinkle the urine on the pile as you build or turn it. Undiluted human urine simply poured on top of a pile may cause odor for a day or two.

Miscellaneous Items

Almost any organic material can be composted, and the avid composter can always find items around the house to add to the compost heap. For example, the contents of a vacuum-cleaner bag are suitable for composting. Cloth products—such as old sheets, towels, clean diapers, and clothing—are also suitable when shredded. Avoid composting fabrics that have chemicals in their finish; cotton is the best bet.

MATERIALS TO FORAGE FOR THE COMPOST PILE

If you want to get into composting in a big way, look beyond your home for compost sources. Materials are available whether you live in the city, the suburbs, or the country. Farms and stables are rich sources of spoiled hay or straw and of various manures. Obtain other materials from grocery stores, factories, mills, restaurants, and retail operations. Only your imagination, dedication, and the size of your vehicle will limit your access to organic materials that can be composted.

Manure

Animal manures are high in nitrogen. Therefore, when they're mixed with a carbon material, such as chopped leaves or hay, they produce a nutrient-rich compost that can be used as a fertilizer. Dried manure is inclined to be richer in most major nutrients than fresh manure. Manure in the form of bedding material, which contains both excrement and urine, is better than just the excrement alone.

Animal manures vary in nutrient value. Chicken manure is among the most nutrient-rich. Don't use fresh chicken manure or horse manure, however; these manures are hot—they burn plants they come into contact with. Cow and pig manures aren't hot and thus aren't likely to cause harm if they're spread around the garden without being well composted. However, it's best to compost animal manure thoroughly if only to avoid the odor.

Manures, especially bedding manures, are likely to contain many weed seeds. If you plan to compost manures, then, use a managed composting system that elevates the internal temperature of the pile to 131° F. (See page 39 for information about managed composting.) This temperature is high enough to kill most weed seeds.

Spoiled Hay or Straw

Straw or hay makes an excellent carbon base for a compost pile, especially in areas where few leaves are available. Hay, which is grown as food for livestock, is usually processed into bales for easy handling, transportation, and storage. Straw consists of the residual stalks from oats, wheat, and other grains that have been harvested and processed. The dried stalks are often baled and used as bedding material for livestock. If either hay or straw gets wet, it loses its value to the farmer. However, this spoiled material is ideal for composting.

Hay contains more nitrogen than straw, but both are valuable additions to the compost pile. Their only drawback is that they may contain weed seeds gathered in the baling process. To kill the weed seeds, the compost pile must have a high internal temperature.

A drive to farming country can almost always turn up a few bales that cost no more

Rather than hinder composting, these fowl contribute to it. Their manure is a fine nitrogen source for the compost pile.

than a dollar or two or may even be free. Watch for fields that have been harvested but contain a few lonely bales. They're probably spoiled, and the farmer will be happy to get rid of them.

Another source of straw is a construction site where the contractor has used bales to control erosion during the earth-moving phase. The contractor is usually happy to give you the straw after the job is finished.

Seaweed or Kelp

If you live near the ocean and harvesting seaweed along beaches and inlets is legal in your area, you have an excellent source of nutrient-rich composting material. In terms of composting, the only concern with seaweed or kelp is the salt content. Wash the salt from plants by letting them sit in a steady rain or rinsing them with water from a garden hose. The more you wash the plants, however, the more nutrients you lose.

Seaweed or kelp can be composted fresh, or it can be dried and then composted. The dried material tends to have a somewhat higher nutrient content. In rainy climates, dry the plants under a protective covering to keep nutrients from leaching.

Industrial or Commercial Waste

The types of waste available to you depend on the industries in your area. Some materials are free, and others may cost a nominal amount. The following are examples of common waste materials, some of which are available only in certain regions.

Corncobs   Shred corncobs before adding them to the pile. Fresh corncobs are harder to shred than cobs that have been exposed to the elements for a few months. Once the cobs have dried, they're a rich carbon source.

For seaside dwellers, salt-marsh hay and seaweed are convenient sources of materials for the compost pile. A caution: Make sure harvesting these materials is legal before you do it.

Cotton waste Mills that process raw cotton produce a great deal of carbon-rich waste. The fabric industry is composting more and more of the waste it produces. However, if you live near a cotton gin, you can probably get—for free—all the cotton waste you want for your own compost pile.

Commercial food waste Restaurants, farmer's markets, and grocery stores are excellent sources of nitrogen-rich food scraps. As with scraps from the kitchen, the trick is to mix the waste with a dry carbon-rich material, soil, or old compost to avoid odors and pests. Avoid meat scraps.

Grapevine waste Each fall, grape orchards and vineyards are sources of carbon-rich material in the form of vine prunings. The prunings must be shredded to be of value in the compost pile, but they have excellent nutritive qualities and produce a soil-enriching compost.

Sawdust If used properly, sawdust is an excellent source of carbon. In the compost pile, it's the perfect complement to nitrogen-rich material. For example, a mixture of fresh sawdust and fresh kitchen waste makes an odor-free compost that is unlikely to attract pests. What's more, sawdust is often available for free.

Some experts contend that because sawdust from black walnut and cedar trees naturally contains toxic chemicals, it shouldn't be composted. Other experienced composters believe that the decomposition process destroys the toxins, but at this point evidence is inconclusive. For now, the best course is not to place black walnut or cedar sawdust on the home landscape.

What Not to Compost

Almost all organic material found in and around the average home is appropriate for backyard composting. Here are a few exceptions.

Coal or Charcoal Ashes
Although wood ashes from a wood-burning stove or fireplace can be valuable compost materials, coal ashes and ashes from a charcoal barbecue contain sulfur oxides and other compounds toxic to the soil. Keep these toxic ashes out of the compost pile.

Diseased Garden Plants
Discard any plants that have died or been pulled because they're diseased. The bacterium, virus, or fungus that caused the disease may survive the composting process and infect the area where you apply the finished compost.

Glossy Paper With Colored Ink
Newsprint, even with color pictures, is an appropriate material for home composting; on the other hand, glossy magazines with color photography are not. The printing industry has made some progress in developing water- or soy-based inks for high-gloss color printing, but most glossy magazines still contain inks that could contribute toxins to the compost pile.

Invasive Weeds
Most weeds are fine additions to the compost heap, but a few exceptions are best disposed of in the trash. Particularly invasive weeds—such as buttercup, morning glory, and quack grass—can survive the low temperatures of a passive pile and live on to infest the composted area. Some weed seeds, such as those of burclover and cheeseweed, have been known to survive the temperatures of even hot compost piles. The wise course of action is to keep compost free of these tenacious species.

Meat and Meat Products
Exclude meat, meat products, grease, and bones from the compost pile unless it's hot and actively managed. See page 44 for techniques for handling food waste.

Pesticide-Treated Plant Material
Exclude grass clippings, weeds, and other plants recently treated with pesticides, unless the plants were soaked by a steady rain after the pesticide application. Although most pesticides break down in the composting process and become harmless, that's not always the case. Assume that the residual effect of the pesticide will last as long in the compost pile as it would on the targeted plant.

Pet Litter
Do not place cat or dog feces in the compost pile. Cat feces can contain parasites that cause brain and eye diseases in children and unborn infants. A cat, especially an outdoor one, can appear healthy but still carry these microorganisms. Most dog feces are probably all right to compost, but the feces of an ill animal could transmit disease. Don't take a chance; discard fecal material.

Making Compost

There are many different ways to produce compost. Choose the basic approach and the techniques that will work best for you.

Describing how to make compost is like trying to describe how to make soup. There are almost as many recipes as there are cooks. Similarly, it's possible to make good compost by using many different methods. The secret to successful composting is to choose the basic approach and the techniques that suit your needs and life-style. Your choices will depend on how deeply you want to be involved in composting—tending a compost pile can take a few hours a year or a few hours a week.

Composting can range from passive—allowing the materials to sit and rot on their own—to highly managed. Whenever you intervene in the process, you're managing the compost to some extent. You can choose to manage a little or a lot. For example, you can either ignore or pay varying degrees of attention to the ratio of carbon materials to nitrogen materials. You can throw uncut materials onto the pile, or you can shred them to encourage faster decomposition. You can install aeration pipes, or you can turn the pile, either once or frequently, to speed up the decay process. As you'll learn, you can intercede in many other ways.

Also, this chapter tells you how to pick a composting site; how to handle food waste; and how to solve problems, such as a pile that smells or doesn't heat up. In addition, you'll find information about other types of composting systems—from sheet composting, to sunken garbage pails, to worm composting.

This secluded composting site, protected from the wind and sun, is just large enough to hold a three-compartment compost bin, garden cart, sifter, and sundry tools.

How you make compost is determined largely by your purpose in composting. If your objective is to process yard waste because the trash collection service no longer accepts it, you may prefer a relatively simple method. On the other hand, if you're eager to produce as much compost as possible to use regularly in your garden, you may opt for a more elaborate method that produces compost faster. If you view composting as an opportunity to get vigorous exercise while producing a valuable product for your landscape, you may choose to be even more actively involved in the process. Finally, if your goal is to produce compost free of most disease organisms and weed seeds, you'll have to manage the pile carefully to get it to the proper temperatures to kill those pests.

Once you've identified your reason for composting, you need to determine your basic approach. Consider whether the passive approach or the managed approach suits your needs and interest. Do this before you get into the practical details of composting.

The simplest passive compost pile consists of heaped waste that is allowed to rot unattended.

PASSIVE COMPOSTING

This approach involves the least amount of time and energy on your part. It requires low maintenance or even no maintenance. You just throw organic materials into a pile and let them rot unattended. There's no need to worry about the technical aspects of composting, such as the carbon-nitrogen ratio.

A passive compost pile takes longer to produce finished compost than an actively managed one. People who choose passive composting aren't usually in a hurry, however. Except in the eyes of true composting devotees, there's little practical difference between compost produced the passive way and compost produced by a more managed approach. In both cases, the finished compost is an excellent soil-building material.

Passive compost piles are one of two types: freestanding or contained. The only reason to put a passive compost pile into a bin or enclosure is to make it neater. The passive pile can easily handle all organic waste except meat

and animal products, and it yields a modest bonus in the form of soil amendment once or twice a year. That's not a bad return for a minimal amount of time and energy.

Creating the Simplest Passive Pile

Collecting organic materials in a freestanding pile is the simplest way to make compost. Although such collections are seldom referred to as compost piles, they exist behind many houses. Homeowners with a little extra land frequently have a pile of organic material slowly decomposing "out back." The collection site is usually the spot where you put organic trash—leaves, grass clippings, brush, and weeds—when there's too much for the regular trash pickup or when there isn't any collection service for that type of material.

With these simple piles no one worries much about insect or animal pests. If the pile smells occasionally, it's usually far enough away from the house so that the odor doesn't bother anyone. These piles are treated as trash heaps; they're seldom mined for the valuable humus that rests at the bottom. It just sits there, enriching the weeds around the heap.

If these organic trash heaps were organized just a little bit, they would be less unsightly and would produce excellent compost. A three-sided enclosure, usually made of chicken wire or concrete blocks, is helpful in keeping the pile neater. With piles of this sort, technical issues such as the carbon-nitrogen ratio of the materials aren't really a consideration. As waste accumulates, it's simply added to the pile.

Perhaps the most important decision is how to handle woody materials. Unless you cut them up, the pile tends to become more of a brush pile than a compost pile. A woody pile decomposes extremely slowly, usually over many years, and becomes enormous quickly. Cutting up the brush with pruners, a machete or—even better—a chipper-shredder keeps the pile compact and allows most of the organic waste to decompose in less than two years.

Don't throw kitchen waste on a simple compost pile. Food scraps attract pests, such as flies, dogs, opossums, raccoons, rats, and skunks. Large amounts of grass clippings or freshly pulled weeds thrown onto a simple pile may smell for a few days, but the odor dissipates fairly quickly.

The Compost Bin or Enclosure

Most home composters are prepared to do a little more than simply throw yard waste into a pile in the back corner of the yard. At the very least, they usually want to enclose the pile. Compost bins or enclosures vary widely in size, design, and type of material. See pages 76 to 85 for various compost bins you can build, as well as commercial models you can buy.

If you take the passive approach to composting, then the size or shape of the bin or enclosure isn't important—it can be as small or as large as you wish. However, if you want to manage your pile, especially if you plan to turn the pile at least once, then the configuration of the container should be considered.

A pile designed to promote fairly fast decomposition must have a volume of 27 to 125 cubic feet. Those volumes represent a cube that ranges in size from 3 feet on each side to 5 feet on each side. If you intend to turn the pile at least once, choose a design that permits access to the pile. If the bin consists of a circle of lightweight chicken wire, the simplest method of turning the pile is to lift up the bin and set it down nearby. Refilling the bin effectively turns the materials. If the bin is heavy or stationary, you need some kind of door or removable sides to provide access for turning.

You can make a compost bin of any durable material that will stand up to the weather. The bin must allow air to reach the pile inside, and some kind of cover is usually a good idea. Certain forms of composting can be done in special containers—for example, composting kitchen waste in a worm box (see page 57).

People who build this type of pile don't usually cover it because they're not worried about rain slowing down the rate of decomposition or leaching nutrients from the finished product. The pile serves more as a yard waste depository than a compost production site.

After a couple of years, a simple compost pile always has some aged compost on the bottom. This material is covered by layers of organic material in less advanced stages of decomposition. After the first few years, most simple piles produce a few cubic feet of finished compost yearly. Remove the finished compost whenever you need it, and keep adding new material to the pile.

MANAGED COMPOSTING

This approach involves active participation, which can range from slightly more effort than is required for the passive method to a major commitment of time and energy. Most home composters find a middle position. They do a little management of their pile but don't pursue composting as a major hobby. The amount of management depends on how fast they want to produce compost and whether they want to kill pathogens and weed seeds.

Putting the organic waste into a bin neatens and organizes the composting area. Here, a multiple-bin setup contains composting materials in various stages of decomposition.

Some books about composting make a distinction between a "slow" pile and a "hot" pile to characterize the involvement of a homeowner in the composting process. However, the concept of managing a pile reflects more accurately the potential for varying degrees of participation in the process. A person who wants to manage a compost pile for any reason— speed of production, efficiency of composting, or exercise—can intervene in the process in many ways.

Whether you have a freestanding or contained pile, decomposition requires four factors: an adequate mix of carbon and nitrogen materials, plenty of air, sufficient moisture, and a population of organisms. These elements can be manipulated in various ways to influence the decomposition process. If you do anything to influence any of the elements, you're managing your compost pile.

In terms of how long producing compost takes, many books make a distinction between a compost pile that is turned and one that isn't. The assumption is that you get compost much faster if you turn a pile and that the process takes a long time if you don't.

This is really a false distinction because management techniques other than turning can speed the process. If you use all the techniques and turn the pile frequently, you can get finished compost in just three to four weeks.

Under ideal conditions, the pile can produce compost just as quickly without being turned. Even if you use only some of the management techniques and never turn the pile, you can still get finished compost quickly—in just 8 to 10 weeks. Choose the techniques that reflect how much you want to intervene in the decomposition process—and that will probably be a function of how fast you want to produce compost.

First, however, you must find a suitable location for your composting operation. Once you've done that, you can start making decisions about how to manage the pile.

SITE SELECTION

Whether your compost pile is passive or managed, choosing where to let the materials rot is an important decision. A managed pile requires attention, and if the heap is relegated to the farthest reaches of the yard, it may soon languish. Even a slow, passive compost heap needs a suitable location to sustain gradual, progressive decomposition of organic matter. Although any pile of organic matter will eventually rot, a well-chosen site can speed up the process.

The first step in choosing a site is to find out about any local regulations pertaining to garbage, waste, or composting. For example, a setback ordinance may be in effect for your area. Or you may be required to compost food waste separately from yard waste. Some towns still have statutes forbidding composting altogether, even though a well-managed compost pile doesn't attract pests or cause other problems. If your municipality has a law against home composting, you may want to organize an effort to educate the local authorities about the benefits of composting and how easily pests can be excluded. In all likelihood, you'll receive encouragement to compost rather than encounter objections.

In surveying your yard for the best place to set up your composting operation, consider the following factors.

Evaluating Proximity to Houses and Patios

Look for a spot that allows you to compost discreetly—as far away as possible from your neighbor's house, patio, and garden. Even a well-managed compost pile may occasionally emit an unpleasant odor. To prevent hostilities with your neighbors, place the composting area downwind from their property, putting distance and visual barriers between the two.

Also plan to place your composting area a comfortable distance from your own house and patio, but not so far away that you'll neglect the pile. Unless you're composting kitchen scraps, the compost pile can be situated anywhere that's reasonably close to the garden or wherever the raw materials will be generated. Place the compost pile downwind from the

Top: This casual compost bin made of wood and wire is hidden among the brush and tall grasses in an out-of-the-way spot at the back of the garden, away from neighbors.
Bottom: No casual observer would suspect that this picturesque grape arbor conceals a compost pile.

house, and tuck it behind a fence, some tall ornamental shrubs, or an evergreen hedge.

If you intend to compost food waste, place the composting area close to the kitchen. Don't forget that kitchen scraps must be taken out in rainy as well as sunny weather. If you can, site the composting area near covered access, such as a carport or garage—the scraps will find their way to the pile on a more regular basis.

Considering Wind and Sun

The effects of wind and sun can either improve or impede the composting process. Microorganisms are responsible for generating and maintaining heat inside an actively managed pile, but the wind and the sun greatly influence heat loss from the exterior of the pile. The more rapid the loss, the less active the microorganisms near the edges of the pile. Hot, dry air also dehydrates the pile, slowing the biological processes in the middle of the heap.

In hot, dry climates, keep the compost pile shaded all day. Piles in hot, moist climates often work best with morning sun to dry some of the excess moisture, and afternoon shade to protect the pile from the intense heat of the sun. Morning sun and afternoon shade is also suitable for compost piles in dry, cool-summer climates. In cool-summer areas with plenty of moisture, a pile benefits from a sunny location to help reduce heat loss and to dry the outside of the pile slightly.

A windy spot in the garden can provide air to a compost pile. Too much air, however, can dry the material, thus hampering the biological process. Compensate for the drying effect of wind by adding water or moving the pile to a more protected spot.

If most of your composting occurs in fall and you want to extend the biological activity further into the cool weather, place the pile in a sunny spot. Conversely, summer composting in many climates is best done in a shady location. When in doubt, do your composting under a large deciduous tree. That way, you'll get the benefit of shade in summer and sun in late fall and winter. Make sure the tree doesn't have invasive roots, which the next section discusses.

Seasonal Compost Schedule

Most people make compost when they accumulate enough organic materials, no matter what time of year it is. Nevertheless, most home composters discover a pattern to the availability of certain ingredients. The vast majority of leaves, a rich carbon source, are available in fall, when nitrogen sources for the compost pile are scarce. Grass and weeds, which provide nitrogen, are available in spring, when leaves aren't. An effective storage system is the key to successfully exploiting the bounties of each season. Then, a simple annual cycle of activities makes it possible to use all the leaves, grass clippings, and other organic materials generated in the yard throughout the year.

Composting in Fall and Winter
In fall, collect fallen leaves and shred or chop them. The primary use for them now is as a mulch for trees, shrubs, and garden beds. Spreading a 4- to 6-inch layer will use most or all of the leaves.

If you have chopped leaves left over, store them in a bin or enclosure for the winter. A 4- by 4- by 4-foot bin can hold the leaves from more than one hundred large trash bags if the foliage is chopped before it's put in the bin. You may have to add the leaves to the bin over time, letting them settle so the enclosure can accommodate them. Some leaf decomposition will take place over the winter, but not a significant amount.

Composting in Spring
In an area with cold winters, spring is the time to start making compost in earnest, since green nitrogen-rich material is available in large quantities. (In a mild-winter climate, you can make compost any time of the year if you have enough carbon and nitrogen materials.) The chopped leaves stored during the fall become the basis for your pile. Build the pile by mixing in weeds, grass clippings, kitchen waste, and other nitrogen-rich materials.

You can collect the leaf mulch and use it in the compost pile, or you can leave it on the ground to decompose slowly as a form of sheet composting (see page 56). Even if you intend to leave the mulch, you may want to pull it off flower and vegetable beds temporarily in early spring so that the sun can warm the soil. Do this about three weeks before the last expected frost.

Spring is a fine time to use up any finished compost left over from last fall. (See the fifth chapter for ways to use compost in the landscape.)

Composting in Summer
This is the time of year that the compost pile is working at its peak rate of decomposition, especially if it has been turned once or twice. If the compost is ready before fall, either begin to use it right away or store it under cover until fall. Start another pile if additional waste materials are available. With enough organic waste, you can produce several batches of highly managed compost during the summer.

Composting in Fall
Late fall is the ideal time to use the finished compost in large amounts around your yard. The annual cycle begins again as the leaves drop and you collect and chop them.

Choosing a Composting Surface

The usual recommended base for a compost pile is bare earth. Uncovered soil allows drainage and the migration of earthworms from underground. A frequent problem, however, is infiltration of the pile by tree roots, which rob the compost of valuable nutrients. Although most trees eventually extend their roots into a nearby long-term compost heap, some trees are particularly aggressive. Trees notorious for stealing fertility include alder, black locust, eucalyptus, redwood, tree-of-heaven, and willow.

If you turn the compost frequently, the tree roots won't make much headway into the pile. However, passive piles may become infested with roots. One solution is to pour a concrete pad for the composting area. Be sure to slope the concrete pad slightly to the back of the pile, so that it drains well and is easy to clean. A lower-cost approach to deterring tree roots is to build the pile on top of large sheets of scrap sheet metal. Another alternative is to compost exclusively in a wood bin with a solid bottom.

Whether you use bare ground or build on a base, the composting area should be nearly level, with just enough slope to the back of the pile to prevent puddling. Make sure the pile drains well so that it's easy to work even after a rain.

Also important, provide plenty of working space around the pile. Allow a minimum access of 6 to 8 feet on at least two sides so that you can use a long-handled pitchfork and bring in a wheelbarrow or garden cart.

MANAGEMENT OF COMPOSTING MATERIALS

Now that you've chosen a suitable location, you're ready to start managing the pile. Management extends to the most basic aspects of composting, beginning with the raw materials you use. You have control over what does and doesn't go into your heap. You can add grass clippings to the pile or leave them on the lawn. You can put chopped leaves in the compost or use them as mulch. You can include chipped woody prunings in the pile or spread them in pathways.

Whatever you use in your pile, make sure you choose as many different materials as possible. A pile made up of various materials is more likely to decompose rapidly and to achieve high

internal temperatures. For example, a mixture of grass clippings, leaves, weeds, brush, and kitchen waste makes a better compost than any of those materials alone. (For materials that work well in a compost pile, see pages 28 to 35.)

Deciding on the raw materials is only the first step in pile management. Your level of involvement in the composting process—and the speed with which you produce finished compost—will be determined by how you collect the materials, whether you cut them up, how you mix them together, and so on. If you use all the techniques discussed on the following pages, you'll have a highly managed system that produces compost quickly. However, there's no need to use all the techniques; pick only the ones that suit you. Your brand of composting may not produce compost as quickly, but it may be just right for your schedule and life-style.

Collecting the Materials

One way to collect composting materials is to throw yard waste into the heap as you clear the waste from the landscape. The pile will grow slowly. If you leave it alone and don't turn it, you can expect to have a layer of compost at the bottom of the pile in a year or two. This strategy requires the least amount of work and maintenance.

Another strategy is to organize a holding area for organic materials until you've accumulated enough to build the pile all at once. Building all at once allows you to mix carbon and nitrogen materials in the right proportions. As a result, the pile will decompose much faster

Even a small urban yard can accommodate a compost bin. This bin is on concrete pavers that allow water to drain through the joints and into the soil.

Handling Food Waste

Properly handled, kitchen waste—even the meat products usually excluded from piles—can be used successfully in a home composting system. However, check local health regulations before composting food scraps, since some municipalities have strict laws governing the disposal of such waste. For example, you may have to compost food scraps separately from nonfood waste. In some areas, you may be required to use a rat-resistant compost bin.

The most common problem in backyard compost piles is an unpleasant odor—and the usual cause is an excessive amount of either grass clippings or kitchen waste. In other words, the problem is too much nitrogen. You can always leave grass clippings on the lawn or use them as mulch to avoid having too much grass in the compost pile, but kitchen waste is a special situation. Stored in a container, especially a covered one, for more than a few days, kitchen waste begins to putrefy and reek. When this occurs outdoors, the food scraps attract flies and other pests.

When you add kitchen waste to a compost pile, be sure to cover it with a carbon-rich material, soil, or old compost to avoid odor and pest problems. Don't include meat, bones, gravy, or fat in a passive pile or one that's seldom turned. Even with a covering of carbon material, meat products usually attract pests.

When you add kitchen waste to a hot, actively managed pile, you don't have to worry about excluding meat products and grease from the pile. The high level of microbial activity can handle those materials—without odors or pest problems. Include bones in the pile if you wish. Although chicken bones and small beef bones won't fully decompose even after a month or two in a hot, managed pile, they'll lose their moisture and become dry and brittle. Add them to the soil, where they'll eventually break down and release phosphorus.

Another way to avoid problems with food waste in a compost pile is to run the waste through a blender or food processor before adding it to the heap. The material will settle down into the pile and won't accumulate on top. The worms and other invertebrates in the outer layers of the pile make short work of this rich food, usually consuming it before it has time to decompose.

Ultimately, the best way to guard against problems is to compost kitchen waste separately in a compost tumbler, worm box, or other system that is designed to handle food.

Assorted ingredients and varying amounts of intervention on your part will all result in compost.

Design a compost pile that reflects your purpose and your willingness to manage the process. If you're not in a hurry, you can throw material into the pile haphazardly. If you're interested in fairly rapid decomposition and high internal temperatures to kill weed seeds, then design the pile with deliberate attention to the carbon-nitrogen ratio (see Proper Mix on page 23).

Achieving roughly equal amounts of carbon and nitrogen is easier if you build the pile all at once. Although layering is traditional, mixing the materials actually works better. To produce a pile that will heat up in less than a day, run alternating handfuls of nitrogen and carbon materials through a shredder as you build the pile.

You can arrange the materials in layers if you wish. The tiers should be between 2 and 6 inches thick. Within that range, the material will heat up in the same amount of time.

As you build the pile, whether you do it gradually or all at once, don't compact the materials in an effort to get more into the composting area. Air is essential to the decomposition process, and compressing the pile just reduces the available air supply and slows decomposition significantly.

Managing the Carbon-Nitrogen Ratio

For home composters, accurate calculation of the carbon-nitrogen ratio of a compost pile is virtually impossible—there are too many variables. However, after you've had a year or two of experience making compost, you'll know when you're on target.

The subtlety of carbon-nitrogen ratios is important only if you're producing compost quickly and want as much nitrogen as possible in the finished product. The difference in the nitrogen content of a compost that decomposed slowly over a year or longer and a compost made carefully but quickly is relatively small. Slow compost protected from the weather may contain between ½ and 1 percent nitrogen; quick compost made with attention to the carbon-nitrogen ratio may contain 2 percent nitrogen.

Feel confident that you're managing the ratio well if you use roughly equal volumes of

---

than a pile assembled gradually. Although you'll produce compost more quickly, you'll have to handle the materials at least twice—once in collecting them for storage and once in building the pile. If you decide to turn the pile, you'll have to handle the materials again.

Building the Pile

Some books about composting give the impression that compost piles must be built according to a particular recipe. They suggest that a pile must be arranged in precise layers of specific materials for decomposition to proceed effectively. This impression is misleading. No single formula provides effective decomposition.

carbon and nitrogen materials and then monitor their decomposition. See Problem Solving on page 51 for advice on correcting an imbalance in the ratio.

Managing Particle Size

The decomposition rate increases as the size of the organic materials decreases. If you don't care about the rate of decomposition, then you can just throw whole, uncut materials into the pile. But if you want the pile to decay faster, take the time to chop up large fibrous materials, such as cornstalks and broccoli stems.

Exclude woody materials if you're not chopping or shredding them, since they take much longer than other organic materials to decay. This is especially important if your compost bin doesn't allow you to pull finished compost from the bottom. Even if there is access space at the bottom, twigs and branches tend to block the way, making the removal of compost a real nuisance.

If buying or renting a shredder makes sense for you (see page 85), give serious thought to getting one. Shredded organic materials heat up rapidly, decompose quickly, and produce a uniform compost. Materials in a compost pile will decompose in weeks rather than months if you run them through a shredder every time you turn the pile.

Monitoring the Temperature

For the enthusiast who enjoys managing the composting process, tracking the temperature in the middle of the pile is not only interesting, but it's important for making management decisions.

The simplest way to track the temperature is to stick your fist into the pile. Another easy method consists of leaving a metal pipe or iron bar in the middle of the pile, then periodically pulling it out and feeling it. If the bar or the interior of the pile feels uncomfortably warm or even hot, you'll know everything is fine. A compost thermometer gives a more accurate reading than fist or pipe and allows you to closely monitor the activity inside the pile.

If the temperature inside is the same as that outside, that's an indication that the decomposition process has slowed down. You may want to spur activity by adding nitrogen-rich material or turning the pile.

Adding Amendments

Some home composters make it a practice to add certain materials—such as limestone, fertilizer, or peat moss—to their compost piles, usually as they're building them. The general assumption is that, by adding substances to the pile, they can influence the nutrient content or the pH of the finished compost. The validity of some of these measures has yet to be proved through research.

Many composters believe that a pile consisting of a large proportion of acidic material, such as oak leaves or pine needles, will yield acidic compost. The goal is usually to offset the acidity, since neutral compost (pH 6.5 to 7.5) is desirable for most plantings. Logic follows that adding an alkaline material, such as limestone or wood ashes, at the time the pile is built will

Top: Woody materials are stored in this old well until they're needed in the compost bin. Bottom: Removable bamboo stakes allow easy access to the composting materials in this bin constructed from shipping pallets. The bin provides the roughly 3- by 3- by 3-foot area needed for efficient decomposition at high temperatures.

Turning the Pile to Produce Compost Quickly

This method is for the composting purist who wants to produce high-quality compost in the shortest possible time. Researchers have learned that decomposition occurs most efficiently when the temperature inside the pile is between 104° and 131° F. They have also learned that it's best not to turn a pile when its internal temperature is in that range. Turn the pile when the temperature is higher or lower.

For best overall results, watch the compost thermometer and turn the pile when the temperature is between 131° and 140° F. Once the pile is hot, turning it causes the heap to cool down, then heat up again. By turning the pile every time it nears the 140° F mark, you keep it operating at its peak. Also, you prevent the pile from getting too hot and killing beneficial organisms.

If the pile contains a variety of materials with a carbon-nitrogen ratio approaching the ideal 30 to 1, then you may have to turn the pile every other day. This method of intervening to sustain the optimum temperature should give you finished compost in about three weeks.

Such a speedy process involves some trade-offs. Although most disease pathogens die when exposed to 131° F for 10 to 15 minutes, some weed seeds are killed only when they're heated to between 140° and 150° F. If you're concerned about weed seeds, then let the pile reach 150° F during the first heating period. Then drop back to a temperature between 131° and 140° F for subsequent turnings. Be aware, however, that temperatures beyond 140° F kill increasing numbers of beneficial organisms in the pile.

Nitrogen-rich food scraps and fresh green plant material are used to balance the carbon content of the compost piles.

neutralize the compost. However, the only sure result of adding limestone or wood ashes to the pile is a greater loss of nitrogen in the form of ammonia gas. Since the premise that compost made of acidic materials will end up acidic hasn't been established, then adding an alkaline material and risking a corresponding loss of nitrogen from the finished product is a questionable trade-off.

If you feel you must add limestone or wood ashes to a pile containing large amounts of acidic materials, add the amendment sparingly. Test the pH of the finished compost to be sure it's acceptable.

Another common practice is to add a general-purpose granular fertilizer to a pile as it's being built and sometimes when it's being turned. The belief is that the fertilizer helps speed the decomposition process and adds valuable nitrogen to the finished compost. Unfortunately, this practice not only doesn't add nitrogen to the final product, but in some cases it actually reduces the amount of nitrogen that would normally have been present.

If your pile consists only of carbon-rich materials—such as dried leaves, straw, or hay—then fertilizer may be helpful in getting the decomposition process started. However, a generous dose of fruit or vegetable peelings can accomplish the same task with no undesirable side effects, such as a loss of nitrogen.

Some books about composting suggest that the nutrient value of compost can be improved by the addition of mineral fertilizers or rock powders, such as rock phosphate or greensand. When added to the soil, these materials break down slowly, releasing their nutrients to plants over months or even years. When these amendments are added to a compost pile, especially to one that heats up to a high temperature once or twice, they're broken down by the decomposition process and their nutrients are released in a soluble form that can be absorbed by plants. However, evidence does not prove that the plants benefit any more from the nutrients released through composting than if the amendment were applied directly to the soil.

Managing the Organisms

The third chapter of this book described the wonderfully complex food chain made up of the hundreds of different organisms found in a typical backyard compost pile. You may ask yourself where these creatures come from. For example, where are the thermophilic bacteria before the pile begins to heat up? All the organic materials in a compost pile already contain, on their surfaces, the various microorganisms needed for the decomposition process. Most of them are dormant and waiting until the environment is right before they become active.

Can you increase the number of organisms in the pile and by doing so increase the speed of decomposition? The answer is yes. Free sources of these microorganisms are readily available, or you can buy a compost activator. The commercial activators contain a combination of microbes as well as enzymes and other natural chemicals involved in the decay process.

However, the simplest way to ensure a generous supply of all the necessary bacteria, fungi, and other microorganisms is to throw a few handfuls of garden soil or old compost—each handful contains billions of microbes—on the pile as you build it. Make sure the pile contains sufficient air and moisture, since the microbes need the right environment to become active.

Most compost piles, especially passive ones, invariably attract invertebrate decomposers, such as earthworms, millipedes, and sowbugs. Even in a hot, actively managed pile, these organisms can be found decomposing material in the outer 12 inches of the pile, which usually remain cool. These creatures show up amazingly quickly, sometimes in just a week or two.

You don't have to depend on nature to supply you with worms, among the most important decomposers in the pile. You can buy fishing worms, usually night crawlers, and add them to the pile. Or you can move earthworms from elsewhere in the yard to the pile. Another alternative is to get special composting worms,

As composting organisms feed on organic waste (right bin), they turn it into finished compost (left bin). To work efficiently, the organisms need plenty of air, sufficient moisture, and the right mix of carbon and nitrogen materials.

Turning a small pile is the simplest, most direct way to aerate it. Periodic restacking of the materials also redistributes the organisms, giving them access to the entire pile.

which require the environment of a compost pile to survive. For more information on using worms in a compost pile, see Composting With Worms, on page 57.

For thorough composting, each type of organism involved in the process must have access to the whole pile over time. The simplest way to accomplish this is to turn the compost pile periodically.

Managing Air

Most of the organisms that decompose organic matter are aerobic—they need air to survive. As the pile decays, the air inside the pile is consumed and the rate of decomposition declines. Bacteria that require less air to function take over. These bacteria work more slowly than aerobic bacteria. That's why a pile that's never turned and doesn't have some other way of gaining access to air takes such a long time to decay.

Techniques for introducing air into a compost pile include turning the pile, making air vents, and using aerating tools.

Turning the pile   Although turning a compost pile offers several benefits, such as redistributing the organisms, the primary benefit is to provide air to all parts of the pile, thus dramatically increasing the rate of decomposition.

Anyone with the right tools and a strong back can turn a compost pile, but a few tricks make the job easier. After a week or two, most compost piles settle by as much as 30 percent; settling is due partly to gravity and partly to decomposition. As the pile sits, it tends to become more dense, compacting as it loses air from the interior. Consequently, a shovel isn't the best tool for turning a compost pile. A composting fork works better because it breaks up compacted material.

The simplest way to turn a pile is to move material from the pile and restack it alongside. With this method you handle all the material just once. For composting systems in which turning the pile regularly is desirable, the best option is a multiple-bin setup. Each time you turn the pile, you just move it to the next bin. A more time-consuming method is to empty the bin and refill it with the same material. That means handling the material twice.

Whichever method you use, the object is to end up with the material that was on the outside of the original pile resting in the middle of the restacked pile. Conversely, the material that was in the center of the original pile should be on the outside of the new pile. This doesn't require great precision. To the degree that you're able to move material around, you'll promote uniform decomposition; the finished compost will have a more consistent texture.

As time passes, the decomposing matter becomes coffee brown and more evenly moist. A 4- to 6-inch layer of gray powdery fungus usually lies under the dry material on the cooler, outer parts of the pile. You can sometimes see steam radiating from the center of the pile as you move the material. As before, try to shift the outer material to the center and the central core to the outside.

Air vents   Many inventive home composters have searched for a way to get air into the middle of a compost pile without having to turn the pile. The solution is to find some device that can be inserted into the pile to allow air to flow to the central core. This section describes a few methods that are reportedly successful.

An easy way to aerate a compost pile without turning the materials is to insert perforated PVC pipes into the heap. The pipes can be inserted horizontally (top) or vertically (bottom).

When building a freestanding compost pile, place two or three sturdy poles across the pile at the halfway point and then again when the pile is three quarters built. The materials will settle in a month or two. To aerate the pile, simply shake the end of each pole every month or so. That movement allows air to pass down the length of the pole. The microbial activity in the area around the poles will increase with each new supply of air. Some composters employ a refinement of the pole-shaking technique. They use bamboo poles split down one side. When the hollow poles are shaken, the splits open a bit, allowing air into the center of the pile.

To get air into an enclosed pile, set a PVC pipe vertically in the center of the pile. Before placing the pipe, which should be at least 1 inch in diameter, drill holes randomly along the length. Load the compost into the bin around the pipe. Some home composters have used three or four aerating pipes set strategically in the pile. An 18-inch length of snow fencing, rolled tightly, can be used instead of PVC pipe.

Another alternative is to build the pile on a wood pallet or on a plastic aeration mat, which is available from some composting equipment suppliers. When you combine a pallet or mat on the bottom of the pile with some kind of a vertical pipe up the middle, you can produce finished compost in only a few weeks—without turning the pile once.

If the composting materials are dry, sprinkle them as you build the pile. Without adequate moisture, the microorganisms no longer feed and decomposition comes to a stop.

Tools for aerating Composting equipment suppliers offer a tool designed especially to introduce air without turning the pile. An aerating tool is a pole approximately 4 feet long. You insert the pole deep into the pile and tug at it, causing the paddles at the end to open. These attachments move the organic materials around a bit, allowing air to get into the center of the pile. The tool works best in a loose pile— you won't be able to insert the pole too far into compressed material.

Managing Moisture

Organic waste needs water to decompose. A pile of dried leaves exposed to rain decomposes in two or three years, whereas the same pile may last for decades if it's kept dry. Too much water, however, is just as detrimental to the composting process as a lack of water. In an overly wet pile, water replaces the air, creating an anaerobic environment. Decomposition slows down.

Ideally, the materials going into a compost pile should have a moisture content of 40 to 60 percent. They should feel slightly moist but not wet—like a sponge after it's been soaked and thoroughly wrung out. The easiest way to achieve that moisture level is to expose the materials to the weather for a month or so. After they absorb some rain and drain off the excess, they'll have just about the right amount of moisture for composting. In an arid climate, use a garden hose to moisten the materials.

If you're using very wet materials, mix them with dry materials as you're building the pile. If all the material is very dry, soak it as you construct the pile. Covering the pile with a plastic tarp, shower curtain, or other impermeable cover helps conserve moisture. An uncovered freestanding compost pile is less vulnerable to oversoaking than a pile inside a container. Rain tends to roll off the sides of a freestanding pile as it does a haystack.

Whenever you turn a pile, check the moisture level and add water if necessary. After a few months uncover a passive pile for one or two rainstorms and then replace the cover. The rain will replace some of the moisture that has been lost to the decomposition process. This solution isn't foolproof, because water may run down the sides without penetrating the center. If there isn't any rain, you can either opt for slow decomposition or sprinkle the pile with water.

PROBLEM SOLVING
Problems in compost piles are relative. The occasional bad odor in a passive pile behind the barn in a rural area may not be considered a problem, whereas the same situation in a dense urban neighborhood may bring the police to your door. The problems addressed here are offered with the understanding that, for some home composters, they may not be serious or require any action.

Eliminating Unpleasant Odor
Bad odor is perhaps the most common problem identified by home composters. No matter the cause, the odor will disappear quickly if you add carbon-rich material, soil, or old compost and turn the pile. The odor will return in a day or two if you just layer the material on top, so be sure to work it into the pile.

To avoid a recurrence of odor, understand that unpleasant smells usually develop because the pile has become anaerobic—it has no air. This may occur when the pile is compacted or when it's soaked with moisture. Turning the pile restores air. Additionally, an anaerobic pile often contains an excess of nitrogen-rich material. Guard against putting too much fresh green material in the pile without adding sufficient carbon-rich material. Also, if heavy rains are likely, cover the pile.

Correcting Dryness
Without adequate moisture, microorganisms cease functioning and decomposition comes to a halt. A sign of this problem is lack of settling. A properly moistened pile shrinks by at least 30 percent in just a month or two. If this doesn't happen, assume your pile isn't moist enough.

The best solution is to turn the heap, applying water with a garden hose as you restack the pile. If you don't want to go to the trouble of turning the pile, however, you can still moisten the pile well enough to spur decomposition. Just pouring water on top of an established pile won't wet the center, because the water will sluice off the outer surfaces. Either turn the garden hose on to a drip and let the water seep

into the pile in various locations, or scoop out a shallow hole in the top of the pile to trap the water. The trapped water will eventually work into the heap. Keep the cover off for one or two soaking rains. If there is no rain, add water with a garden hose once or twice more.

Correcting Wetness
The only cure for an overly wet pile, no matter the cause, is to turn the pile while adding carbon-rich material, soil, or old compost. Any of these materials can help absorb the excess moisture and keep the pile from putrefying. If you do nothing, the wet pile may start to smell. And, since it lacks air, the material will take at least a year to decompose.

Increasing Heat
Except during cold weather, the center of a compost pile should be uncomfortably warm or even hot to the touch. If the center is only just warm,

Top: Finished compost is completely covered to prevent the rain from leaching nutrients.
Bottom: The right-hand bin containing raw materials is loosely covered to conserve the moisture content.

check first to see if the pile is adequately moist. Decomposition slows down in a pile that's either too dry or too wet (the preceding paragraphs present solutions for both problems).

If the moisture level is correct, the most likely cause for the lack of heat is that the pile is too small. Unless the pile is at least 3 by 3 by 3 feet, it doesn't have enough critical mass to support the microbial activity that will generate the high temperatures associated with efficient decomposition.

If the pile is adequately moist and large enough, the problem may be a deficiency of nitrogen-rich material. Add fresh, green material and turn the pile.

Preventing Freezing

Most composting microorganisms become inactive below 40° F, although psychrophilic bacteria work in temperatures as low as 28° F. Decomposition continues at a slow rate even in colder weather, since the interior of a compost pile is always warmer than the air temperature. However, a moist pile that isn't covered

The best way to keep flies away is to cover food waste and fresh manure with a generous layer of soil, old compost, or a carbon-rich material such as sawdust.

can freeze during a cold winter. Logic seems to indicate that turning the pile would spur microbial activity and heat up the compost material, but doing so will actually accelerate the heat loss. Keep the pile warm by covering it with clear plastic, which serves as a solar heating mechanism. If the pile freezes despite covering, don't worry; the decomposition process will resume in spring.

Precluding Flies

Houseflies and fruit flies around the compost pile indicate that the pile isn't properly built or maintained. Rather than dealing with them once they become a problem, prevent the pests by using correct techniques from the start.

Unless you treat food waste properly, it'll attract flies. The same is true of fresh manure. Whenever you add either to the pile, cover it with carbon-rich material, soil, or old compost. A tarp or other covering over the whole pile isn't a substitute and won't keep out flies.

If the flies have already arrived and maggots are present, turning the pile may eliminate

them. Make sure that the material on the outside of the pile, where the eggs and maggots are, ends up inside the restacked pile. The heat in the interior of the pile will kill the pests.

If you choose not to turn the pile and you're not prepared to tolerate maggots, release natural predators, such as parasitic wasps and predatory nematodes. The latter will control a maggot problem in a matter of days.

Precluding Animal Pests

Sometimes, home composters have problems with cats, dogs, opossums, raccoons, and even rats around the compost pile. Here again, preventing these pests is preferable to coping with them after they arrive.

None of these animals will be a problem if the pile is built and maintained properly. Animals whose habitats are nearby may not even be aware of the pile if you take the basic precautions: Add a layer of carbon-rich material, soil, or old compost over food waste. The topping keeps the pile from smelling and attracting animals.

If animal pests are a particular problem in your area, choose a bin that denies access to the creatures. A strong cover on the bin will deter pests if they're inclined to investigate the pile.

THE FINISHED COMPOST

Commercial composting operations have a fairly precise definition of what constitutes finished compost. When ready to use, the compost has a carbon-nitrogen ratio of approximately 15 to 1, has undergone a volume reduction of about 50 percent, and shows a weight reduction of about 50 percent. For homeowners, the decision to start using the compost they've made is more subjective.

Knowing when backyard compost is ready to use is as precise as knowing when homemade chili is ready to eat. It's done when you believe that it's done. Finished compost is usually dark brown or black and resembles commercial potting soil, although it may be much coarser. Even when the finished compost is lumpy, all the ingredients have lost their individual identities.

The appearance of finished compost depends largely on the raw ingredients. In most cases, the end product is a rich dark brown or black earthy material that may be crumbly or dense. To get a looser, more finely grained product, sift the compost.

This homemade sifter turns clumps of compost into a crumbly material ready for spreading in the garden.

If you prefer quantitative measures of doneness, you may want to conduct a temperature test, although it involves some effort. First, turn the compost pile. Then record the temperature inside the pile after it's had a chance to heat up. The test is effective only if you take the temperature after you introduce oxygen by turning the pile. A temperature that doesn't exceed 110° F is a sign that microbial decomposition has finished.

The outside layers of the pile don't usually decay completely, but compost doesn't have to be fully decomposed to be useful around the yard. For example, coarse compost that's only 50 percent decomposed can be used as a mulch or soil amendment anywhere in the garden. It'll continue to break down slowly, but it won't generate enough heat to harm plants. However, if you need compost for a potting mix, make sure it's completely decomposed.

To produce a uniformly textured, fluffy product, run the finished compost through a shredder. You can also sift the compost if you need very fine material for starting seeds or to mix with peat moss for container plants.

Store extra compost in a protected spot or under a tarp. Compost exposed to rain or snow will lose many of its nutrients, although it will still be a valuable soil amendment.

OTHER APPROACHES TO COMPOSTING

Most homeowners compost waste in a free-standing pile or in an enclosure of some kind. However, you may want to consider the following approaches, some of which are particularly effective in handling kitchen waste.

Using a Compost Tumbler

This type of composting device offers some of the advantages of a managed composting system without requiring as much effort—as long as you can easily turn the crank. A compost tumbler is usually cylindrical or barrel-shaped and has air vents in the sides. As you collect waste materials, you dump them into the tumbler. When you fasten the door and crank the handle, the tumbler turns, mixing the materials and aerating them. When a tumbler is loaded and turned every day, it produces finished compost in about one month.

The primary disadvantage of a tumbler is its small size. Even the largest tumbler can't handle the volume of yard waste that can be processed in an average-sized bin or enclosure.

On the other hand, a tumbler is particularly effective as a dedicated device for composting kitchen waste. Load the tumbler with chopped leaves in fall to provide a basic supply of carbon, then routinely dump in kitchen scraps every few days and turn the crank four or five times. The food waste decomposes without smelling bad. If the tumbler is used exclusively for kitchen waste, it doesn't fill up quickly and can function for up to six months before requiring a renewed supply of carbon materials. When composting is completed, distribute the finished product around the yard, then add another batch of chopped leaves to the tumbler and start the process all over again.

A grammar school in Massachusetts is using four medium-sized compost tumblers to process cafeteria waste. The tumblers also serve as teaching devices. Every day during the first week, the children place food scraps in the first tumbler and give it a turn. During the second week, they put waste in the second device and turn both tumblers. The sequence continues until all the tumblers are filled and turned. After the fourth week, the material in the first tumbler is finished compost, and the children distribute it around the school's shrubs and trees.

Composting in Sunken Garbage Pails

Another composting system designed to handle just kitchen waste requires two 5-gallon garbage cans. They can be made of either plastic or galvanized metal, as long as drainage holes can be punched or cut into the bottoms. The bottoms can be cut off if desired. Bury each can in the ground so that the rim protrudes 1 or 2 inches above the soil level. Allow enough of a protrusion so that each cover can be tightly secured.

Once the cans are installed, dump all kitchen waste, including meat products, into one can until it's full. This process may take months, since the material settles considerably. Although a tightly covered can emits no odor, expect a strong smell when you remove the lid to deposit more waste. In addition to trapping odor, the tight cover prevents insects, dogs, and cats from bothering the operation.

When the first can is nearly full, throw in a few handfuls of garden soil and keep the lid tightly shut while the other can fills up. When the second can is full, the first can will yield finished compost free of odor and insects. Most weed seeds will be killed.

Some people keep a third garbage can alongside the two buried ones to store sawdust, soil, or old compost. Each time they put food scraps in the can, they add a handful or two of the stored material to suppress odor.

A tumbler is an ideal vehicle for composting food waste. Every time you crank the tumbler, in effect you are turning the pile. Daily cranking can produce finished compost in about a month.

Sheet Composting

This is a way to dispose of waste and get the benefits of decayed organic matter without building a compost pile. The techniques of sheet composting range from spreading the organic waste directly on the soil, to digging it under, to liquefying it and pouring it around plants. Mulching with an organic material is nothing more than sheet composting at its simplest—the organic material breaks down slowly and is pulled into the soil by earthworms and other soil life.

A sheet compost decays in place and then is worked into the soil. Constructed in a vegetable or flower bed in fall or winter, the sheet compost produces a soil-enriching amendment by spring.

Sheet composting on the surface   The most common type of sheet composting involves layering organic waste over a garden area and tilling it in with a hoe, spade, garden fork, or rotary tiller. Almost anything that goes into a compost pile can be sheet-composted. Leaves

are the ideal organic material, since they're easily tilled into the soil and decompose rapidly. Grass clippings, manure, and food waste (except meat and meat products) are also effective materials. The best course is to shred or chop the material before you layer it.

To sheet-compost in fall, spread a 4- to 6-inch layer of organic materials on the soil surface. To do it in spring, spread a 2- to 3-inch layer about a month before planting time. If you don't have enough nitrogen materials, you may want to spread some granular fertilizer at the same time to help stimulate the decomposition process. Throw handfuls of soil over the sheet compost to ensure sufficient microbial activity to process the waste. Then work all the material into the soil. A tiller is the best tool to work compost material into a vegetable garden. In a flower bed, where you don't want to disturb perennials and bulbs, work in the organic material carefully with a garden fork or hoe.

If you sheet-compost in fall, the organic materials will have largely decomposed and blended into the soil by spring planting time. A sheet compost started in early spring won't be as thoroughly decomposed, but you'll be able to plant after four or five weeks.

The double-digging technique   If you plan to double-dig a garden bed as a way of preparing the soil for planting, you can incorporate sheet composting into the process. Double digging consists of scooping out a trench about 1 foot wide and 1 shovelful deep across the bed, loosening the soil at the bottom with a garden fork, then replacing the top layer of soil.

To incorporate sheet composting, add a 2- to 4-inch layer of organic material after loosening the soil at the bottom of the trench. This added step effectively raises the bed a few inches and improves drainage. The added organic waste breaks down slowly, leaving the soil loose, friable, and more fertile.

Although double digging requires considerable physical effort, it need only be repeated every few years. For best results, double-dig in fall to give the organic waste time to decompose before spring planting.

Buried waste   You may prefer this technique if most of your garden is always planted, making surface composting or double digging difficult or even impossible. Dig 6-inch-diameter holes near shrubs and other perennial plants; the holes should be 12 inches deep. Into each hole deposit shredded or chopped yard waste or kitchen scraps. Refill the holes, burying the waste. When you collect more waste, dig more holes and fill them. This is an effective method for disposing of limited quantities of organic material.

Liquefied food waste   Kitchen scraps, except meat products, can easily be turned into liquid form for use in sheet composting. A heavy-duty blender or food processor can reduce rinds, peelings, and other waste to a purée that can be poured directly onto garden beds and around trees and shrubs. The purée decomposes where you pour it. Gardeners who compost this way report no odors or pest problems. The technique also eliminates the need for fertilizer in areas where the liquid waste has been applied. Within about two weeks the material is pulled into the soil by earthworms and other soil organisms.

Composting With Worms

Worms are remarkable composters. Various kinds of earthworms find their way into any compost pile in contact with bare soil. They work their way around the outer areas of the pile, consuming organic material and processing it through their bodies. In a passive pile of leaves, the worms do as much work as microorganisms in the year or two it takes to turn the pile into compost. When organic waste is left on the soil surface, earthworms are involved to a large extent in breaking the waste down and pulling it into the soil.

You can use worms as a composting tool. Add worms to a pile outdoors, or set up a worm box to handle kitchen waste. Be sure to distinguish between ordinary earthworms and composting worms, which are highly specialized for composting duty but don't usually survive elsewhere.

Earthworms perform valuable services in the compost pile. Their castings constitute a superior nitrogen-rich fertilizer—the more earthworms in a compost pile, the richer the finished compost. Earthworms secrete calcium carbonate, a compound that helps to moderate soil pH. As earthworms move around a pile, they rearrange and loosen the compost materials, improving aeration. Their tunnels provide

a way for other organisms, such as sowbugs and millipedes, to get deep into the pile. Like earthworms, these organisms contribute to the decomposition process.

Composting worms—known variously as red worms, red wigglers, red hybrids, and manure worms—reproduce much more rapidly than common earthworms. They process more organic material than earthworms simply because they multiply so quickly. It takes just 8 red worms to produce 1,500 new red worms in only six months. Since they don't usually survive in the home landscape, however, they must be purchased each season. Two types of composting worms are commonly sold: *Eisenia foetida* can't live in the soil at all, and *Lumbricus rubellus* can sometimes survive in the soil. A pound of red worms (about 1,000 to 2,000 worms) typically costs between $10 and $15.

Worms in a compost pile   Worms are useful in helping to speed up decomposition in any compost pile, although obviously they aren't practical in piles that are run through a shredder. They're most valuable in passive compost piles that are just left alone to rot. Either earthworms or composting worms can cut the decomposition time of a passive pile by at least 50 percent.

Composting worms are much more efficient than common earthworms. One pound of composting worms added to a compost pile in late spring can make a noticeable difference in the speed of decomposition. Unfortunately, composting worms are so voracious that they literally eat themselves out of work. Once they digest most of the organic material in the pile, they're in danger of starving to death. To keep the worms going, transfer them to a fresh pile of organic waste promptly.

Unlike earthworms, composting worms stay above the soil and don't hibernate. Therefore, they usually die if they're left in a pile during the winter in the North. If you want to protect composting worms, devise a holding box for them in the basement, garage, or other location where the temperature stays above freezing.

Worm boxes   Although raising earthworms in a worm farm in the home is difficult, the composting worm is suited to life in a box. Some people keep a worm box the year around to process the family's kitchen waste, including

Top: By reproducing prodigiously, composting worms are able to process raw materials faster than earthworms, which breed more slowly. Bottom: Periodically remove finished compost from a worm box and replace it with shredded newspaper or another bedding material.

meat scraps. Others simply use a worm box to hold composting worms during the winter so that they can form the nucleus of a new population for the outdoor compost pile in spring.

Composting worms prefer a temperature range of 55° to 77° F, making a heated basement, garage, attic, or sunroom a likely site for the worm box. In mild-winter climates, the box can probably stay outdoors all year, but be sure to bring it indoors if you expect a cold snap.

A properly managed worm box won't smell or attract insects. However, if conditions get out of balance, flies may appear or odors may develop. As this section will explain, the problem disappears when the factors are brought back into balance.

Your first step in planning a worm box is considering its size and shape. The size depends on how much waste you intend to process. The rule of thumb is to provide roughly 1 square foot of surface area for each pound of food waste produced per week—for example, 7 pounds of kitchen scraps per week requires about 7 square feet of surface area, or a box about 2 by 3½ feet. The container should be from 8 to 12 inches deep to avoid compaction.

The number of worms in the box determines how much waste you can process. About 2,000 composting worms (roughly 2 pounds) can process 7 pounds of kitchen scraps in a week. Two pounds of worms for every pound of waste is a standard ratio. If you generate about ½ pound of kitchen waste daily, then 1 pound of worms should be sufficient to do the job. Remember, composting worms multiply quickly to cover any increase in waste.

The worms need an organic bedding material, such as shredded leaves, newspaper, cardboard, or peat moss. Add a few handfuls of garden soil to the bedding mix to introduce microbial decomposers to the box. As the bedding material decomposes along with the kitchen waste, it will become dense and air access will decrease proportionally. You may have to add bedding material to ensure that the worms get enough air.

To survive, composting worms need an environment consisting of about 75 percent moisture. Weigh the bedding material, then mix it with water equal to three times that weight. If you have 4 pounds of bedding material, then add 12 pounds of water. Since 1 pint of water weighs 1 pound, that means adding 12 pints, or 1½ gallons, of water. Thoroughly moisten the bedding material before adding the worms. Most worm farmers cover the worm box with a sheet of black plastic or a wooden cover to keep in moisture and keep out light.

Follow a pattern in adding kitchen waste; once you have deposited material to a particular spot, don't disturb that area with new waste for about a month. Chopping the waste is unneccessary, but it'll break down faster if you chop it. Some people chop the scraps in a blender, drain off the liquid, and add the solids to the worm farm. Whenever you add waste, chopped or not, cover it with bedding material.

Every two to four months, renew the worm box by adding new bedding and removing some or all of the finished compost. The easiest method of doing this is to remove one half of the material, including the worms, and spread it out in the landscape as compost. The worms will die, contributing further to the compost. Use fresh bedding material to fill the space made available by removing the finished compost from the box. If you don't add any new waste to the old bedding material, the worms will migrate to the new bedding in three to four weeks. Then you can remove the other half of the old material, including any worms lagging behind, and replace it with new bedding. The worm farm is now good for another few months.

Another method is to separate the worms from the bedding by exposing the worm box to light. The worms will move toward the middle, away from the light. As you scoop off the composted material in the outer parts of the box, the worms will collect in an even tighter group in the center. Add fresh bedding after you remove the compost.

If you keep the box indoors through the winter, move it to a shady, protected spot outdoors in spring. As an alternative, dump the worms onto the compost pile and set up the worm box again in fall.

Composting Anaerobically

Most of the composting techniques discussed in this book are aerobic—they depend on the availability of air. However, due to bacteria and other microorganisms that are able to function without air, decomposition can occur in an anaerobic environment. A noxious smell is the telltale sign of anaerobic composting. Many homeowners have inadvertently experimented with anaerobic composting when they seal plastic bags full of grass clippings and let the bags sit for a while.

The anaerobic approach to composting can be practical for small amounts of material if you take care to keep bad odors from escaping. Some commercial composting bins designed to handle food scraps, such as kitchen waste digesters, work anaerobically. (See page 85 for more about these digesters.)

Another common device for anaerobic decomposition is a large plastic bag into which you put organic materials, such as leaves, grass clippings, and even kitchen waste. Add a few handfuls of soil to spur microbial activity, or use a compost activator intended for plastic-bag composting. If the materials in the bag are dry, then add water to make them moist but not wet. Secure the bag and place it in the sun to heat up. Turn the bag every week or two, not because it needs air, but to mix the materials and expose all sides to the heat of the sun.

There's no way to predict how long this process will take to produce compost, but you can start to check for a finished product after a few months. If the material is very wet and smells bad, add dry material and tie the bag up again for another month or two. Continue to turn the bag regularly. Compost produced this way is similar to compost produced aerobically.

Using Compost

Considering its myriad benefits, homemade compost may be the most useful means you have of maintaining a healthy landscape. Distribute it wherever you want to improve the soil quality.

O nce raw composting materials have decayed into a dark, rich substance that looks and smells like humusy soil, you're ready to start using the compost. But—where and how? There are many ways to use this valuable material. A basic understanding of how compost benefits a home landscape will help you make effective use of your compost supply.

Compost is an outstanding source of organic matter that can be dug into the soil to improve structure, aeration, water retention, drainage, nutrient quality, and other soil properties. A soil regularly amended with compost is easy to work, and—as home gardeners who regularly use compost can attest—it fosters healthy, vigorous plants. In addition to being dug in, compost can be spread on the soil surface to act as a mulch.

Most home composters don't produce enough of this wonderful substance to use it everywhere they want to. Therefore, prioritizing its use is important. This chapter tells you how to do that and explains how to use compost in various parts of the landscape, such as new planting areas, existing garden beds, and lawns. It explains how to make compost tea, a dilute fertilizer, and how to use compost to fight pests.

Dug into the soil, compost has a remarkable effect on both sandy and clayey soils, making them more workable and productive.

A vegetable garden benefits from generous additions of compost at planting time. The compost gets the plants off to a good start and provides a steady nutrient supply throughout the growing season.

THE BENEFITS OF COMPOST

Adding organic matter is one of the best things you can do for your soil—and homemade compost is among the best sources of organic matter. Inexpensive to produce and easy to use, backyard compost serves primarily as a soil conditioner, whether it's spread in a layer on the soil surface or is dug in. A garden soil regularly amended with compost is better able to hold air and water, drains more efficiently, and contains a nutrient reserve that plants can draw on. As a result, almost all plants growing in compost-amended soil are healthier and more productive than they would be without compost. The exceptions are native plants that prefer unamended soil and some drought-resistant plants that may be damaged by the addition of such water-retaining material.

This section details some of the major benefits of using compost. When you add them up, you'll find that compost is one of the most valuable resources home gardeners have for maintaining a healthy landscape. The joy of digging in rich, workable soil and tending healthy, flourishing plants will more than compensate for the effort you expend in making the compost and distributing it in the landscape.

Improved Soil Structure

When a source of organic matter, such as compost, is worked into the soil, either by people or earthworms, it dramatically improves the soil structure—the arrangement of sand, silt, and clay particles that make up soil.

How does a handful of your soil feel? Are the particles so fine that they pack together tightly, leaving little space for air? If so, the soil is probably clay soil, which becomes gummy when wet. Clay soils feel heavy, dense, and solid. Are the soil particles in your hand large, coarse, and light, their looseness creating so much air space that water drains through them quickly? This coarse texture is typical of sandy soils.

Between those two extremes is loam. It contains small and large pores, so that it holds water and air yet drains well. What gives loam its distinctive properties is the presence of humus, or decomposed organic matter. Humus helps soil particles stick together in larger groups, or aggregates, giving the soil a granulated, crumbly property described as friable. Consequently, to the degree that a clayey or sandy soil can be amended with humus-rich material like compost, it becomes more like the ideal soil, loam.

Increased Microbial Activity

Even though the decomposition process in compost has slowed down, billions of microorganisms remain in every handful of the finished material. When you incorporate compost into the soil, you add the microorganisms as well. They reinforce the resident microbial population, increasing their activity.

As the microorganisms continue to decompose organic matter in the soil, they contribute to the chemical reactions that benefit plants.

They convert nitrogen, phosphorus, potassium, calcium, and other nutrients in organic materials into a form that plants can absorb. Some of the microorganisms are nitrogen-fixing bacteria, which take nitrogen from the air and make it accessible to plants. Other microbes manufacture antibiotics that protect plants from various diseases.

Increased Nutrients

Like other sources of decomposed organic matter, compost contributes valuable nutrients to the soil. If you're using compost as the mainstay of your fertilizing program, think in terms of adding inches, not a fraction of an inch. Most home composters don't produce enough finished material to rely on it as their only fertilizer source. Still, whatever can be added provides a valuable reservoir of nutrients that plants can draw on over time.

The nutrient content of a given batch of finished compost is impossible to predict, since it depends on such variables as the raw materials, the carbon-nitrogen ratio of the pile, and whether any amendments are added. For

When added to the soil, mature compost continues to decay, gradually making nitrogen and other nutrients available to plants.

Compost improves the overall health of most plants and strengthens plant resistance to insect pests and diseases.

In addition, compost contains certain acids, which are formed as by-products of decomposition. These acids help to break down some of the rock particles in the soil, releasing nutrients that would otherwise be unavailable to plants.

Improved Soil Chemistry

Soils exhibit a tremendous range of conditions from nutrient excesses or deficiencies to extreme alkalinity or acidity. Organic matter, such as compost, fosters a soil chemistry that avoids these extremes.

For example, organic matter increases the buffering capacity of soil—its ability to resist a change in pH when acidic or alkaline materials are added.

In addition, organic matter bonds to certain micronutrients—such as iron, zinc, copper, and manganese—increasing their availability to plants. In soils low in organic matter, these micronutrients are often tied up. Even though the nutrient is present in the soil, plants may show symptoms of a deficiency, such as yellowing or poor growth.

Moderation of Soil Temperature

Plants are sensitive to the temperature of the soil in which their roots are growing. Regardless of the air temperature, seeds germinate only when the soil temperature warms up to a certain level. For instance, peas germinate when the soil is at least 45° F, and no sooner. The root systems of most plants grow best when the soil temperature is between 65° and 85° F. When it rises above 85° F, most plants simply stop growing; they just sit there until the soil cools. How does this relate to compost?

Soil amended with compost typically has a darker color than unamended soil, since most compost is dark brown or black. A dark soil absorbs more heat from the sun than a light soil. Consequently, garden soil amended with generous amounts of compost tends to heat up faster in spring, stimulating plants to start growing sooner in the season.

During hot weather, soil mulched with 1 to 2 inches of compost remains cooler than soil with no organic mulch. The mulch serves as a blanket, protecting the underlying soil from the sun. If soil temperature can be kept below 85° F— that point at which plant growth stops—the plants will perform better in the summer heat.

example, compost made from hay contains more nitrogen than compost made from straw, and composted manure contains significantly more nitrogen than either.

Fresh compost that hasn't been exposed to rain contains nitrogen, phosphorus, potassium, and many of the trace minerals needed by plants. Compost that has been left out in the weather—or even stored covered for more than six months—has lost some nitrogen and potassium, although it still retains most of the other nutrients. About one half of the nutrients in compost are released for plant use during the first year. One half of the remaining nutrients are released during the second year, and so on after that.

Compost also serves as a ready food source for the billions of soil microorganisms that convert the soluble compounds in compost into a form that can be absorbed by plant roots. Many compounds in compost supply the microorganisms with oxygen, which is essential to their reproduction.

Improved Plant Health

Most plants growing in soil amended with a good source of organic matter, such as compost, will look better and perform better than plants in unamended soil. Here's a brief look at how organic matter added to the soil ultimately yields sturdier, healthier plants. If you regularly add compost to your soil, you won't have to water and fertilize as often, and you'll spend less time struggling with plant problems.

General plant health   A soil well amended with organic matter fosters a moderate but steady rate of root growth for most plants. Uniform growth is a result of the consistent supply of water, air, and nutrients that the amendment helps supply over time.

Growing plants with a consistent supply of organic matter is better for plants than growing them in a soil low in organic matter and then applying a fast-acting nitrogen fertilizer to spur growth. A fertilizer-induced growth surge tapers off in a few weeks, as the nutrient

supply is depleted. Then the plants are left to cope with reduced levels of nutrients until the next dose of fertilizer. This on-again, off-again growth pattern stresses plants, causing them to fall short of their best performance. This pattern also makes them more vulnerable to insect pests and diseases.

A well-amended soil holds moisture, which plants can absorb according to their particular needs. Plants with steady access to water are healthier and more vigorous than plants with a fluctuating water supply.

Insect and disease resistance   Research indicates that a soil to which compost is added regularly tends to produce plants with fewer insect and disease problems. Two reasons explain this phenomenon. First, the compost encourages a more active and larger population of beneficial soil microorganisms, which control harmful microorganisms. Second, compost-amended soil fosters healthy plant growth, and healthy plants are better able to resist pests.

These vegetable and flower beds contribute organic waste to the wire bin composter and then profit from the rich soil amendment produced when the waste decays.

Using Compost to Fight Pests

Compost can be used to combat certain pests, including parasitic nematodes and fungi. Compost whose temperature didn't exceed 140° F during the decomposition process has more pest-fighting ability than compost that reached higher temperatures. Increasing numbers of beneficial organisms are killed as the temperature rises, and the compost may be sterile if the temperature of the pile goes above 160° F.

Nematode Problems

Research has shown that leaf mold compost, or compost made exclusively from dried leaves, can suppress harmful nematodes. Although many different kinds of partially decomposed leaves are toxic to nematodes, pine needles have been found to be particularly potent. For the best results, mix about 1 inch of leaf mold compost into your soil to a depth of 6 to 8 inches. Apply yearly to maintain control.

Disease Problems

Compost has properties that make it effective in controlling certain plant diseases, especially fungus diseases.

Wherever compost is spread in the landscape, it helps reduce fungus problems just by virtue of its presence on or in the soil. At the same time, there are some specific tricks for using compost as a disease fighter.

Fungus problems on lawns Some of the common lawn diseases—such as dollar spot, brown patch, and fusarium patch—can be treated with compost if treated when the disease first appears. As soon as symptoms are apparent in patches or sections of the lawn, spread a ½-inch layer of compost over the infected area. Don't water for a few days. Then, if no rain has occurred, lightly water the affected area during the morning so that it'll dry before nightfall. If the fungus disease persists for more than two weeks, you may decide to use a fungicide to deal with the problem.

Fungus problems on indoor seedlings Compost can reduce problems with damping-off, a common fungus disease of seedlings started indoors. Suppress the damping-off spores by mixing compost into the seeding mix. An effec-tive mixture consists of equal parts of compost, vermiculite, and perlite or coarse sand. Make sure air circulation is adequate, since damping-off seldom attacks a well-ventilated seedling. The best way to ensure circulation is to set up a fan to blow a very light breeze over the flats or pots of newly sprouted seeds.

Tree injuries For centuries, those with a special feel for the land would treat a wound on a tree with a handful of soil. Studies indicate that the microbial content of compost has similar disease-fighting capabilities. If a tree has been wounded by a lawn mower or a weed trimmer or has suffered damage from wind or storms, a poultice of compost is as effective a treatment as you can find to keep out disease until a callus forms over the injury. Dampen the compost slightly and lay it on the wound, taking care to cover the entire injured surface. Secure the compost with a tree wrap or some other biodegradable material, such as a cotton cloth. After a few months, when the tree has formed a callus, remove the wrap if it hasn't already rotted away.

It's a fact of nature that insect pests and diseases strike the weakest plants first.

When compost is used as a mulch, it helps control the spread of fungus diseases by keeping water from splashing disease spores onto plants. For this reason and because studies indicate that compost-rich soil discourages many fungus diseases, mixing compost right into the soil around plants vulnerable to those diseases can protect the health of your garden.

Some composts, particularly those made from animal manures, tend to suppress harmful root-invading fungi. Research has shown that harmful soil fungi responsible for diseases such as root rots and damping-off are controlled by other soil organisms. The presence of microbe-rich compost ensures that large populations of beneficial bacteria and fungi are present, thereby reducing the likelihood of disease problems.

Other research has revealed that, in many cases, compost made the slow, passive way has better disease-resisting ability than actively managed compost, which is produced more quickly and under higher temperatures. The reason is that high temperatures kill beneficial organisms. If the temperature doesn't exceed 140° F, most of the desirable microbes can survive. However, the compost may become sterile if the temperature goes much higher—for example, above 160° F. You can rescue a batch of high-temperature compost by mixing it with small amounts of mature compost made at lower temperatures; the resulting material will offer disease resistance.

COMPOST ALLOCATION

Considering the benefits of compost, the only complaint most home composters have about it is that they never seem to have enough. Spreading a ½-inch layer as a topdressing on a 5,000-square-foot lawn requires around 200 cubic feet of compost. It would take several large bins filled to the top to produce that amount of finished compost. Most people will never be able to make that much compost in a season even if they reduce their yard waste close to zero. For that reason, prioritizing the use of the compost supply is important.

Top: Planting wells are filled with composted manure, which will be worked into the soil. Bottom: Strategically placed compost produces an excellent growing environment for perennials.

How Much to Use

Most books and articles dealing with compost simply advise you to spread the material around a garden bed or plant. They seldom offer any guidance on how thick the layer should be. As a result, most people waste their compost by spreading it too thick. Unless you're relying on compost as a fertilizer, spread no more than 1 inch. A thicker layer doesn't harm the soil, but it does limit the total area that can be improved.

If your supply of compost is severely limited, consider stretching it by mixing it with an equal amount of dried leaves, municipal compost, or other organic materials available locally.

Compost doesn't last forever once it's in the soil. It continues to decompose as microbial action converts it into plant nutrients, so eventually the percentage of organic matter in the soil begins to decline. In northern climates, compost is mostly decomposed after two years in the soil. In southern climates, compost disappears even faster and should be replenished every year.

Where to Use Compost

Deciding where to use your compost should be based on how much you have. If you have a limited amount, then you'll want to make sure you get the greatest impact from it. For those lucky enough to have a large supply, prioritizing its use isn't as important.

Since compost builds good soil, the first priority for a limited supply is probably an area where the soil quality needs the most attention. Is that area the highly visible flower bed in the front of the house? Is it the vegetable garden because the size and quality of the harvest are important? Is it a prized tree or shrub? Decide where you want the soil to be superior. That's where you'll use the compost.

New planting areas   The soil in a newly established garden bed is usually inferior, especially if it was previously under a lawn. Unless the lawn was top-dressed regularly and grass clippings were left on it to decompose, the soil probably lacks organic matter and may be compacted as well. Compost can condition the soil and elevate it to a quality that will sustain healthy plants.

The soil around new homes is usually quite poor. Typically, the contractor scrapes off and hauls away the topsoil before building the house. Often, instead of replacing the topsoil, the contractor brings in inferior soil when the house is completed. Regular additions of compost can improve the soil.

It takes more compost to remedy an inferior soil than to maintain soil health. To bolster poor soil, spread 2 to 3 inches of compost over the newly dug surface. Then work the compost into the top 6 to 8 inches of earth. Digging deeper isn't necessary, since most feeder roots tend to be near the soil surface.

Existing planting areas   A garden soil that has been well mulched and amended periodically requires only about a ½-inch layer of compost yearly to maintain its quality, although you can use more if you wish. A garden soil that needs frequent watering and produces fewer crops or less vigorous plants than usual may contain an insufficient amount of organic matter. In that case, it may be necessary to add a 1-inch layer of compost for a year or two to rehabilitate the soil.

Late fall, when many plants are dormant or have been pulled, is the best time to spread compost over a garden bed. Don't bother working the compost into the soil; just spread it on top and cover it with a winter mulch, such as chopped leaves. By spring, soil organisms will have worked the compost into the soil for you. If spring is the only time you can spread the compost, then work it into the soil a few inches. Otherwise, the compost may dry out in the sun.

If your supply of compost is really limited, consider side-dressing, a way to use compost sparingly by strategically placing it around certain plants or along certain rows. Side-dressing is more economical than spreading the compost uniformly over the soil.

Side-dressing is best done in late spring and early summer so that the rapidly growing plants can derive the maximum benefit from the compost. To side-dress a plant, lay a circle of compost on the bare soil around the plant. Start it about an inch away from the stem and spread it out to the drip line (the soil beneath the outer edge of the foliage). Scratch the compost into the soil with a trowel or hand cultivator, taking care not to disturb the plant roots. For shallow-rooted plants, such as azaleas and many annual flowers, leave the compost on the soil surface and let the rain, earthworms, and other soil organisms take it below the surface.

Side-dressing—placing an amendment on or in the soil around plant roots—is an effective way of stretching a limited supply of compost.

At first, side-dressed compost that sits on the soil surface awaiting transfer into the soil acts as a mulch. As a temporary mulch, it's most effective when at least 1 inch thick. A 2-inch layer works even better. Partially decomposed compost is ideal for this purpose. Not only is it still slowly decomposing, but it usually has more volume than finished compost and thus covers more area.

New lawns If you intend to plant a lawn where the soil is in poor condition or has been compacted by construction activities, you'll need a 2- to 3-inch layer of compost. If the soil is heavily compacted, you may need to use a rotary tiller to work the compost into the soil at least 6 to 8 inches. Once the new lawn is established, spread a ¼- to ½-inch layer yearly to maintain the quality of the soil.

In addition, compost can play an important role when you start a new lawn where one previously existed. Either remove or kill the existing lawn. Spread a 1-inch layer of compost or a mixture of compost and other organic matter over the area. One alternative is to use a rotary tiller to dig in the compost. This process does, however, churn up weed seeds. Once the seeds are exposed to light and air, they germinate and compete with the grass seeds.

A better alternative is to aerate the soil after you kill the existing grass. An aerating machine punches small holes in the dead turf, simultaneously pulling out plugs of soil. Spread a layer of compost over the area. Instead of incorporating the compost, lightly rake it so that it falls into the holes. Then plant the new grass. Not only does this approach take much less work and avoid bringing dormant weed seeds to the surface, but it has the added benefit of introducing air into the soil.

Existing lawns A lawn top-dressed with a ½-inch layer of compost every year or two will be healthier and will require much less fertilizer and water than an unamended lawn. Fall is the best time to apply the compost, although an application in early spring is almost as effective. The best way to get the compost into the soil is to aerate the lawn either before or after you spread the material. If aerating isn't possible, the compost will still find its way down below the surface of the soil—the earthworms and microorganisms near the soil surface will carry it down within a few weeks.

Trees and shrubs A compost mulch can benefit trees and shrubs just as it does other plants. (For information about mulching, see page 15.)

Spread compost over bare spots in a lawn before reseeding. Top-dress the lawn— spread a thin layer of compost over the entire expanse—every year or so if your compost supply is large enough.

Compost made from manure and sawdust is used as a mulch over apple tree roots.

A circle of mulch is particularly useful around trees and shrubs in a lawn; it protects them from lawn mowers and weed trimmers, as well as reduces the competition from surrounding grass plants for food and water.

Spread a ½- to 1-inch layer of compost on the bare soil under the tree as far as the drip line (the soil beneath the outer edge of the foliage). The compost will protect any roots that are protruding because of compacted soil. As the compost breaks down and moves into the soil, it becomes available to the vast network of feeder roots near the soil surface. If a ground cover surrounds the tree, sprinkle compost among the plants to condition the soil for them and the tree.

When you spread compost on bare soil, cover it with a 2- to 3-inch layer of some other kind of organic mulch, such as chopped leaves, pine needles, or wood chips. The mulch will

hold the compost in place and keep it from drying out. If such a mulch is already in place and is too difficult to remove, just lay the compost on top. The rain and soil organisms will work it into the soil.

Mulching a large tree takes a considerable amount of compost. Home composters often reserve some of their compost supply for trees that have sentimental, historical, or horticultural value or that need extra care because of injury or illness. To get maximum impact from the compost, use fertilizer. The only truly effective way to fertilize trees is to inject nutrients into the soil the way professional arborists do. In the soil under the drip line and, if possible, 1 or 2 feet beyond, drill 1- to 2-inch-diameter holes. The holes should be 18 inches apart and 12 inches deep. Fill the bottom one third of each hole with a slow-release all-purpose granular fertilizer, and top off the holes with compost.

This treatment will provide steady sustenance to a tree for two to three years. Under a shrub, drill the holes only 8 to 10 inches deep.

Trees suffer from problems other than a lack of nutrients, of course. One such problem is surface rooting. Sometimes, homeowners try to hide surface roots, which look unsightly and may present a hazard, by shoveling soil on top of them. Unfortunately, this harms the tree and may kill it. To cover the surface roots of trees safely, use a very light soil mix and spread it thinly over the area. Mix equal parts of soil and compost, then spread a 2-inch layer over the roots. A thicker covering will smother the exposed roots, which have become accustomed to getting oxygen. Replenish the covering as needed. Aerating the soil beneath the tree is also helpful.

Flower and vegetable transplants One of the best times to use compost, especially if your supply is limited, is when you're transplanting flowers, vegetables, and other small nonwoody plants. However, don't use compost in the planting hole when you're planting trees and shrubs. Most gardening books in the past recommended the practice, but recent studies have found that a compost-rich soil mix around the roots of a newly planted tree or shrub encourages the roots to remain in the planting hole rather than venturing out into the surrounding soil. The roots grow in a circle and, after a few years, the plant literally strangles itself and dies.

Adding compost to the planting hole gets smaller perennial plants off to a good start, however. Compost is particularly valuable for perennial food plants, such as asparagus, rhubarb, strawberries, raspberries, and blueberries. Even annuals benefit from a dose of compost at planting time.

When you dig the hole, throw in a handful of compost before positioning the plant. The compost provides nutritional support throughout the season, and it improves the soil structure around the plant. If you make it a practice to add compost whenever you plant, you'll greatly improve the soil over time. Areas where annuals are set out every season will have especially good soil after a few years.

Containerized plants Most plant experts recommend a soilless mix for houseplants and outdoor plants in containers. Garden soil isn't considered suitable for potting applications because its quality is so variable—it may be heavy and drain poorly, or it may be loose and unable to hold water. Additionally, garden soil may contain disease organisms, weed seeds, and insect eggs.

Soilless mixes usually consist of peat moss, perlite, and vermiculite. These ingredients ensure that the growing medium is light and airy and that it holds water while draining well. However, soilless mixes don't have any nutritional component. To provide some nutritional support for plants and to introduce microbial activity, add compost to a soilless mix. A mixture of 2 parts soilless mix and 1 part screened compost provides a high-quality environment for plants. If you want to include garden soil, a suitable mixture consists of equal parts of garden soil, screened compost, and sand.

Lavender is planted in a mound made up of leaves, wood chips, and other organic waste and covered with 6 inches of topsoil. The waste gradually decays into a nutrient-rich, humusy material that supports healthy plant growth.

Top: Regular applications of compost in vegetable and flower beds encourage sturdy, vigorous plants. Bottom: Make compost tea by wrapping compost in a burlap bag and suspending the bag in a tub of water. Use the mild brew to fertilize young plants.

However you use the compost in soil for a container, remember that the compost will be used up eventually, just as it is when you mix it into a garden bed. Therefore, apply fertilizer regularly.

Compost tea New transplants and young seedlings are sensitive to chemicals, so applying fertilizer to them often does more harm than good. Compost tea is an effective way to supply sensitive plants with a safe dose of nutrition. The infusion is a convenient way to add nutrients to the soil in planters, as well—growing areas that sometimes lack space for the addition of a solid soil amendment.

To make compost tea, fill a sturdy burlap bag with fresh compost and tie it at the top so that it resembles a tea bag. Suspend the bag in a tub or a barrel of water for a few days. The water leaches nutrients from the compost and dilutes them into a mild tonic the same color as tea. Use this liquid as a soil drench, pouring it directly on the soil at watering time. The same bag of compost can produce several batches of compost tea.

OTHER SOURCES OF COMPOST

There are so many uses for compost that it's tempting to try all of them. If you can produce only a limited supply in your backyard, however, you won't have enough to go around. Fortunately, compost is available through sources other than your own compost pile, so you can stretch your supply. The following are a few types of compost found in many regions; other equally effective materials may be available in your area.

Municipal Compost

Since so many states have passed legislation excluding yard waste from landfills, communities across the United States are setting up their own composting operations. Leaves, grass clippings, brush, and other organic materials are still collected by the trash pickup system, but they end up at a composting site instead of a landfill. In most cases, the materials are laid out in huge windrows hundreds of yards long. Large machines designed to turn compost move down the windrows every few days, turning the piles.

The municipality uses the compost in public areas, such as parks, athletic fields, and landscaped areas around public buildings. A large percentage is sold to the nursery industry, usually at a reasonable cost. Often, there's still compost left over for use by residents. In some communities, the compost is offered free to locals who are willing to pick it up.

Composted Sewage Sludge

Sewage, the liquid effluent from industry and the toilets of private residences, presents as serious a disposal problem as trash. Again, composting promises to diminish the problem. Hundreds of cities have already undertaken programs to compost sludge, the solid residue from sewage waste. The finished product is a dark, humus-rich material suitable for use in residential landscapes. In the coming years many more cities are expected to institute similar programs.

The composting procedure varies somewhat from city to city, but the basic approach is similar. After the sludge emerges from the sewage treatment plant, it's mixed with wood chips and composted at high temperatures to kill disease organisms. When the composted mixture is dried and cured, the large wood chips are screened out. Since composted sewage sludge tends to have a higher organic content than homemade compost made from yard waste, its benefits usually last longer in the soil.

For many years, composted sludge wasn't considered safe for use in home applications because of concern about heavy metals that might prove toxic in home landscapes. The heavy-metal content of the sludge was primarily a problem in industrial areas, and regulations limiting metal pollutants entering the sewage system have reduced that problem. People may wish to avoid using composted sewage sludge on vegetable gardens just to be absolutely sure, but in most cities the heavy-metal content of the finished product is well below safe tolerances for all home applications.

Composted sewage sludge may be available directly from a municipality or from the utility responsible for sewage treatment, or it may be sold through garden centers or soil yards.

Mushroom Compost

Home gardeners in some regions have access to another excellent source of humus—the medium in which mushrooms are grown, or mushroom compost. Mushrooms are grown in a mixture of straw and manure, which is no longer suitable as a growing medium after the mixture decomposes. The spent bedding, which is either sold directly by mushroom farmers or is marketed through garden centers or soil yards, makes an excellent soil conditioner.

To be sure that the manure won't burn plants, let the mushroom compost age for at least six weeks before using it in your garden. Mushroom compost put through a shredder with homemade compost makes a wonderfully soft, uniform material that can be used anywhere in the home landscape.

Treated sewage sludge is mixed with wood chips and then composted in large aerated piles at East Bay Municipal Utility District's composting site in Oakland, California. The compost is dried, cured, and screened before it's sold for landscape use.

Choosing Equipment

This chapter will help you narrow your choices: whether to build or buy a bin and what kind of tools to obtain.

In the past, people who wanted to set up a composting operation in the backyard may have had trouble finding the right equipment. Now—thanks to the intense interest in recycling—the marketplace abounds with home compost bins and other composting tools and supplies.

The equipment you choose will depend on the amount of waste you have and the composting techniques you use. The simpler your system, the fewer tools you'll need. For example, you can make compost just by heaping uncut materials into a freestanding pile and allowing them to rot on their own. For such a simple system, you don't need much more than a shovel or fork. If your pile is highly managed, you may want two or more bins, some kind of shredding device, and such accessories as a compost thermometer and a garden cart.

This chapter will help you decide whether to construct a bin or buy one. For do-it-yourselfers, there are instructions for building bins from shipping pallets, wire fencing, concrete blocks, or railroad ties; also included is a detailed plan for a three-bin system made from wood and wire mesh. For people who want to buy, there's a review of commercial composting devices, including compost tumblers and wire, wood, and plastic bins.

You'll also find information about cutting and shredding equipment, including mulching mowers, leaf shredders, and chipper-shredders. To choose the right fork or other tool, look in this chapter for the section on tools and supplies.

A sturdy garden cart can transport large quantities of compost throughout the garden. A cart is able to hold up to three times as much material as a wheelbarrow.

The type of equipment you'll need depends on your composting method. Although you can produce compost without a bin, most home composters find that some type of container makes the process easier and keeps the area neater. For actively managed composting, many experienced composters use two or more bins. If you turn your pile regularly, get a quality garden fork. If you want to track the temperature of the pile, you'll appreciate a compost thermometer. To transport a large volume of finished compost, a garden cart may be a necessity.

The equipment you choose will also depend on the amount and type of waste you have. You may not need any special equipment if your property generates a limited amount of waste that you process in a slow, passive pile. If you have a large volume of waste and want to produce compost quickly, you may find some kind of shredding machinery helpful.

First, consider whether you want to build your own bin or buy a commercial bin. You may

Compost bins made from shipping pallets are functional, even if they don't win any beauty contests. Here, the pallets are wired together and braced with boards.

decide not to have a bin at all—for instructions on building a freestanding architectural compost pile, see opposite page.

BUILDING A COMPOST BIN

Constructing your own bin offers many advantages over buying a bin. You can save money, especially if you use scrap materials. You can make the bin any shape, and it can be as simple or as elaborate as you want. Most important, making your own bin allows you to compost large amounts of material at high temperatures. Most commercial bins don't hold the minimum volume—approximately 3 by 3 by 3 feet—needed for a hot, actively managed pile. (For information about buying a compost bin, see page 81.)

Home gardeners are constantly inventing creative and inexpensive ways to hold their compost—for example, bins made from wire mesh or from shipping pallets. For all the designs described in this section, you'll have to figure out the volume that best suits your situation. Estimate the bulk of the raw materials that you expect to collect. If you've been setting the yard waste out on the curb in plastic garbage bags, just calculate the total by considering the typical load for one week.

If you don't have enough experience with the raw materials to calculate the total, simply guess. If you miscalculate, you can make another wire cylinder or pallet bin quickly and inexpensively. Except with relatively expensive materials such as cinder block and railroad ties, it pays to overestimate the volume from the start so you don't get caught short of composting space.

Note that many of the models that this section lists have no provision for excluding rain or water from sprinklers. To keep the compost from getting too wet, use a tarp or a wood or metal lid to cover the bin.

Pallet Bins

Resourceful home composters long ago discovered the usefulness of the shipping pallet in composting. They found that building a compost pile on top of a pallet is an effective way to aerate the pile (see Managing Air on page 48). Fastened together, pallets also make a serviceable compost bin or storage bin.

Made from wood slats nailed to a reinforcing frame, pallets are strong enough to contain

Building an Architectural Compost Pile

By arranging the composting materials carefully, you can build an architectural compost pile—a tidy freestanding pile that has vertical sides and will heat up to high temperatures. This approach represents the true art of composting, combining the biology of decomposition with an architect's attention to detail. You don't turn this type of pile; the interior achieves high temperatures because the pile consists of a sufficient mix of materials and is arranged for maximum air infiltration.

Begin by laying a 1- to 1½-foot-thick base of both woody and nonwoody garden clippings; spread the material 4 to 6 feet wide by whatever length you desire so that you can easily reach the center with a pitchfork. Insert a wood post every 2 to 3 feet down the middle of the longest dimension of the pile. After the pile is constructed, you'll remove the posts; the holes will serve as air inlets and heat vents.

Around the edge of the pile, loosely fork an 8- to 14-inch-thick layer of straw, hay, tall grass, or semiwoody annual weeds. The edging should be approximately as wide as the pitchfork. Make sure that some of the strands of the edging material extend into the central section of the pile. Fill the middle with a mix of carbon and nitrogen materials, moistening them if necessary.

Next make another berm of strawy material around the outside edge of the pile, directly on top of the previous edging. If the sides start to taper in toward the middle, pull the berm back upright by inserting the prongs of the pitchfork vertically into the edging and carefully dragging it toward the outside.

Continue forming layers around the perimeter and filling the middle of the pile until you reach the desired height. Remember, the pile must have enough critical mass for efficient decomposition. A cube shape, such as 4 by 4 by 4 feet, is ideal. Even though this type of pile sheds water well, cover it anyway. If any of the material on the outside of the pile doesn't decay because it's too dry, shave it off and use it for the middle of your next pile.

For a simple bin, fashion a length of fencing into a cylinder and fasten the ends with wire. This bin, made from turkey wire, holds organic waste until it's added to the compost pile.

Snow fencing, a readily available material in cold-winter climates, makes an effective bin. The fencing is made from 1½-inch vertical wood slats wired together so that a 2½-inch gap separates each slat. This configuration helps hold in the composting materials while giving them access to air. Snow fencing comes in rolls 3, 4, or 6 feet wide.

To build a snow-fence bin, drive metal fencing stakes into the ground in a circular pattern. The stakes should be the same height as the snow fencing. Wire one of the cut ends of the fencing to a stake, then attach the fencing to the remaining stakes, leaving 3 to 4 feet of the other cut end of the fencing free. Wire the end loosely to the first stake so that you can easily unfasten the flap to gain access to the bin.

Concrete- or Cinder-Block Bins

Make a relatively simple, three-sided bin by stacking concrete or cinder blocks. Leave the fourth side open for turning the pile or for access to the finished compost. One advantage of not using mortar is the ability to vary the length and width of the bin to accommodate large or small quantities of raw materials. In addition, blocks allow you to easily construct more bins as needed.

Since you'll be stacking heavy blocks, be sure to build on a firm, level surface. You can use an old patio, part of the driveway, or a concrete pad you've poured just for this purpose. If you build on bare ground, pick a spot with level, compact soil and tamp the area.

The blocks are laid like bricks—they're staggered to overlap the seam between the blocks on the lower course. You can buy half blocks to fill the gaps at the ends of courses caused by this staggering. Your local supplier can quickly figure how many blocks and half blocks you'll need by looking at a simple sketch with the dimensions labeled. Don't build the walls any higher than 4 feet.

Place the blocks with the hollow centers facing up. If you like, leave a gap of several inches between blocks to help aerate the pile, although compost material may eventually fill these gaps. Start the bottom course with a full block in each corner and continue laying blocks to form the walls. Use half blocks to fill in the short gap at the end of each wall, and start alternate courses by laying a half block.

a compost pile but also have gaps that help aerate it. Pallets are usually free for the taking when they become splintered or damaged in some other way.

Some gardeners simply lash together four pallets, leaving one corner loosely attached to act as a door. Other gardeners install posts in four corners, nail the pallets to the posts to form three sides of the bin, and wire the last pallet with some slack to allow access.

Wire Cylinders

Fencing or wire mesh makes a fine compost bin, as long as the holes are small enough to hold in the raw materials. A circular bin is usually the most attractive, sturdiest, and easiest to install. A wire cylinder also makes a practical holding bin for raw materials you're collecting for the compost pile.

Wood and Wire Three-Bin System

This sturdy, spacious multiple-bin system made of wood and wire mesh is designed to provide the air circulation essential for efficient decomposition. Each bin can hold slightly more than the minimum volume required for a hot, actively managed pile. You can use the first compartment for the daily collection of organic waste; the second for the working compost pile; and the third for finished or nearly finished compost.

The structure will last longer if you use naturally rot-resistant wood, such as cedar or redwood, or pressure-treated lumber.

All the materials—except the filler strips (part F) and the removable boards (part H)—can be precut to the lengths called for in the materials list. Start construction by joining parts B and C. Note that the 2 by 4s of the 2 inside dividers are attached along an edge.

Join these subassemblies by nailing on all the boards, part D. Remember to leave a 1-inch space at the front (see detail in illustration). After you add the filler strips, part F, you'll have a groove for the removable boards to slide in. Nail on part E to cover the opening left by the 2 bottom boards. Then attach part A to form the base of the bins.

Space the dividers as shown in the illustration, then add the 3 back boards, part G. Hold the pipes snugly against the front of the dividers, keeping them centered. Drive the pipes into the ground with a sledgehammer. Add the pipe clamps, using large panhead sheet-metal screws instead of conventional wood screws. Line the inside of the bins with wire fabric, securing it to the wood frame with galvanized fence staples.

Materials List

A = four 5-foot lengths of 2 by 6
B = eight 34½-inch lengths of 2 by 6
C = eight 34½-inch lengths of 2 by 4
D = eighteen 54½-inch lengths of 1 by 6
E = two 47½-inch lengths of 1 by 3
F = stock length of 1 by 2, cut to suit
G = three 9-foot lengths of 2 by 6
H = optional number of 1 by 6 boards, cut to suit
Four 6-foot lengths of ¾-inch galvanized pipe
12 pipe clamps with panhead sheet-metal screws
About 45 feet of galvanized wire fabric, 36 inches wide
1 package galvanized fence staples

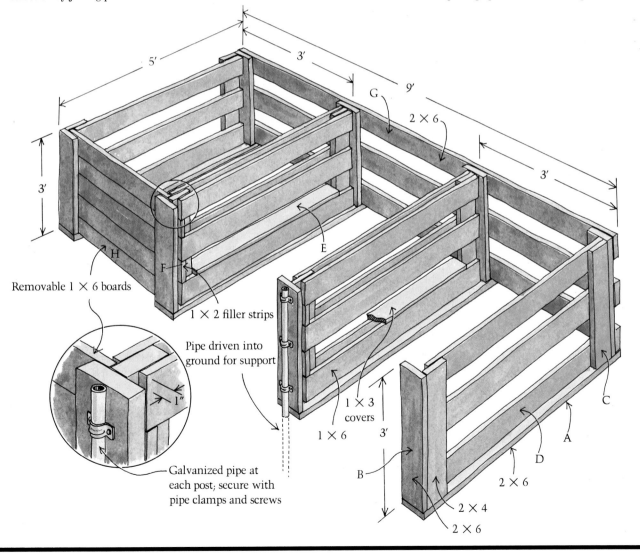

Removable 1 × 6 boards

1 × 2 filler strips

Pipe driven into ground for support

Galvanized pipe at each post; secure with pipe clamps and screws

1 × 3 covers

1 × 6

3'

2 × 4

2 × 6

These easy-to-make wood compost bins are constructed like log cabins. Use logs, straight branches, or bamboo stakes.

If you're building on bare ground, use a carpenter's level to make sure the top of the first course is level and the subsequent courses are plumb. Whether you build on soil or on a paved surface, use a carpenter's square to check the corners.

Railroad-Tie Bins

Railroad ties are excellent for making a large compost bin, providing the cumbersome timbers can be delivered to your property or you have someone to help you transport them.

A railroad-tie bin consists of three sides and an open end, much like the concrete- or cinderblock bin described in the preceding section. The ties are 8 to 10 feet long and usually require some cutting to make them fit the bin size you want. A chain saw is the best way to cut a railroad tie, although the gravel, sand, and dust embedded in the cracks of the wood quickly grind down the sharpest chain saw blade. If you rent a chain saw, be prepared to pay for a damaged chain. Wear long pants,

heavy work shoes, safety glasses, ear protection, and gloves. Don't wear loose clothing that could get caught in the chain.

Lay the ties log-cabin fashion so that they overlap in the corners. To stabilize the walls, pound a length of ½-inch concrete-reinforcing bar, or rebar, every 2 to 3 feet along the outside of the walls; use large metal staples to secure the tie to the rebar.

Another stabilizing option involves drilling a ¾-inch hole every 2 to 3 feet along the top of the first course. On each subsequent course, drill holes to line up with the ones on the previous level, then pound either rebar or ½-inch galvanized metal pipe through the aligned holes. You'll need to rent a heavy-duty reversible drill with an auger bit on a shaft long enough to penetrate the thickness of the tie. The drill should have both a D handle and a side handle to prevent the action of the drill from twisting your wrists.

Whether you drive the stakes along the outside of the walls or insert them through holes in the ties, make sure they're flush with the tops of the railroad ties. By doing so, you'll prevent scrapes and puncture wounds later.

BUYING A COMMERCIAL COMPOST BIN

You may want to purchase a bin if you're not concerned with cost or if you're not handy with tools and want a ready-made structure. Fortunately, the renewed interest in recycling has prompted a great increase in the types of composting systems available commercially.

You need to shop carefully to find the right equipment for your needs. The sales literature doesn't usually list the limitations of a particular product or mention where it may be inappropriate. Even when a company advertises more than one type of composting system, discerning why anyone would want to buy one system rather than another is often difficult. This section will help you cut through the confusion. By recognizing the virtues and limitations of each type of product, you can choose the best one for your yard, budget, and life-style.

The first caution is that most commercial composters are smaller than 3 by 3 by 3 feet, or 27 cubic feet—the minimum volume for an active, managed system under ideal conditions. You may need an even larger bin if you intend to compost under less than ideal conditions. For example, if you're building a pile in Michigan in late November, you may need to mound the material 5 feet on each side to insulate the middle.

Keep in mind that many commercial composters have no provision for excluding rain or sprinkler water. To keep the compost from getting too wet, you'll need to cover it with a tarp or a wood or metal lid.

Before buying any system, ask the manufacturer or the retail outlet for names of people in your area who have bought the system. Find out how well the composter works for them. This is especially important when you're evaluating one of the more expensive or complicated models. Also, read about the models you're investigating. Most gardening magazines periodically review composting devices; look in the yearly index under "Compost."

These commercial composting bins include both wood and plastic models.

Commercial models include a wire bin (top), a three-compartment wood bin with removable front slats (center), and a log-cabin–style wood bin (bottom) with metal rods that you lift to gain access to finished compost.

Simple Wire Containers

Portable, economical, and fairly easy to assemble, a simple wire bin is often the beginning home composter's choice. Tidier than an unrestrained heap, wire bins hold from 15½ to 23½ cubic feet. For some models, you can buy panels that allow you to make additional bins or to change the configuration and make a single, larger bin. Wire bins are available in different shapes—square, round, pentagonal, and hexagonal. The bins can also serve as places to bank raw materials for the compost pile.

All wire bins use galvanized metal mesh made from 7- to 14-gauge wire, and some have the added protection of PVC coating. Buy a model with a high gauge number, since the higher the number, the larger the diameter of the wire and the greater the strength of the constructed bin. Beware of buying a bin with a low gauge number, because the sides may bow out when filled with anything but the lightest material. Check to make sure the bin can be opened and refastened easily.

Individual wire bins cost from $35 to $60. Extra panels, available for some models, range from $20 to $40.

Wood Bins

Two types of wood compost bins are available commercially. One type has solid boards fixed on three sides and removable planks on the unloading end. The other type has long, thin slats stacked horizontally like a log cabin and secured with metal rods through holes in each corner. Both types come unassembled.

If you plan to turn the pile, look for a model that allows you to remove all the boards from one side. Some bins allow you to harvest finished compost from the bottom of the bin, but the design makes it difficult to turn the pile from above.

Many of the bins can hold nearly the requisite volume for actively managed composting; different models have volumes ranging from 20 to 29 cubic feet.

Although wood bins give a natural, rustic look to a garden, they have some serious limitations compared to bins made from plastic, wire, or other materials. They're vulnerable to gradual decay as the composting bacteria slowly eat away at the wood. Make sure the model you buy is made from rot-resistant wood, such as cedar or redwood. If you decide to use a preservative to further slow the decay, avoid wood preservatives containing arsenic or pentachlorophenol.

Another limitation of wood is that it warps and twists easily when exposed to the weather for a long period of time. The log-cabin bin is especially prone to warping. This makes reinserting the metal rods difficult. Even bins made from solid boards can twist enough to make them difficult to open or shut.

Some wood bins come with boards for the top, but rain will just seep in the cracks. You'll still need to supply a tarp for complete protection.

Prices for log-cabin models range from $85 to $150. Solid-board bins cost from $110 to $225.

Plastic Bins

Plastic bins are longer lasting, more lightweight, and easier to move than wood bins, and long-term exposure to the weather won't cause them to warp. Most have a capacity of only 12 cubic feet, although you can find models ranging from 14 to 32 cubic feet.

Look for a model with an ultraviolet inhibitor, which will make the plastic last much longer in direct sunlight—although, ultimately, any plastic bin will weaken and break down. You may also want to shop for a model made from recycled plastic. When the time comes for you to get rid of the bin, however, you may not find any recycling centers in your community to accept it.

Top: This type of plastic composter, which resembles a garbage can, is a familiar sight in the utility area of many urban yards. Bottom: This inexpensive plastic cylinder makes an effective compost bin. Don't rely on the holes to aerate the pile—to get air into the middle of the pile, you'll have to turn the materials, make air vents, or use an aerating tool.

Most models have a sliding panel near the bottom to make harvesting finished compost easy. Make sure the panel opens and closes easily. One model comes apart in three sections that can be stacked in reverse order when you turn the pile.

The catalog copy for many plastic bins mentions that the bin has insulating walls for heat retention and holes for ventilation. Realistically speaking, these models can't provide heat retention and air circulation at the same time, especially in cold weather.

A new type of plastic bin consists of a mesh cylinder with a solid plastic cap, called a dish, on the top and the bottom. The bin is rat resistant, since the lip of the dish fits snugly around the cylinder and the mesh has ⅜-inch holes. To turn the pile, remove the top dish and flip it over so that the lip faces up; unfasten the carriage bolts that keep the front of the cylinder closed, then reassemble the cylinder on the former top dish, refill the bin, and secure the remaining dish. The plastic mesh bin is available in 12- and 21-cubic-foot models.

Plastic compost bins cost from $50 to $150.

Compost Tumblers

Most tumblers hold less waste material than bins—the smaller models range from 7 to 11 cubic feet, and the larger models hold up to 22

Top: This commercial plastic composter comes apart in three sections. Turn the pile by restacking the sections.
Bottom: The composting materials are turned by rotating the metal bin.

cubic feet. However, convenience and rapid decomposition—in as little as three weeks for some models—are their advantages. Every time you rotate the drum, you're turning the pile. This type of composting device is often used for food waste and is positioned outside the kitchen door.

Wet composting materials are much heavier than they look, as becomes evident when you actually use a compost tumbler. Some people have trouble rotating the drum, even one with a gear mechanism intended to make turning easier. A tumbler that spins around its long axis may take less effort to turn than a model that rotates from top to bottom, a maneuver requiring the operator to squat. Look for a model that's easy to turn and convenient to load and empty.

You must pay close attention to the moisture content of the raw materials, since some tumblers tend to keep the material too wet for ideal composting and others dry it out too quickly. Also, compost tumblers seem to require more attention to achieving the proper carbon-nitrogen ratio than bins.

Compost tumblers range in price from $110 to $380.

Kitchen Waste Digesters

Among the newer devices are plastic composters that you bury partway in the ground. One type—green and cone-shaped—is intended solely for processing kitchen scraps; the other type—black and bell-shaped—can be used for kitchen waste and small amounts of grass clippings. Both types work anaerobically, or without air.

A kitchen waste digester isn't really designed to produce finished compost. It's meant to keep kitchen waste out of community landfills by allowing it to putrefy over a long period of time. Much of the material rots away; the rest persists as a dark earthy material that usually isn't as crumbly or uniform as compost produced aerobically, or it collapses into a slimy lump that you bury. A kitchen waste digester is best suited to someone who wants to get rid of kitchen waste without throwing it into the trash but is too busy to garden, is unable to handle a large pile, or doesn't need the extra compost.

Since the digesters are buried, they aren't suited to soils with a high water table. The

This green cone-shaped device, which processes food waste, should be buried partway in the ground.

bottom basket on the cone-type digester was designed to be rodentproof. To protect the bell-shaped device from rodents, line the inside of the hole with wire fabric before setting the unit in the ground. The bell-shaped composter tends to attract flies; to discourage them, throw in a handful of soil every time you add waste. With a large household, the digesters sometimes fill up within four to five months, and the smells released when removing the device and burying the waste can be quite repugnant.

A kitchen waste digester will cost from $100 to $125.

CHOOSING CUTTING OR SHREDDING EQUIPMENT

Before buying any cutting equipment, consider whether it's essential to your style of composting. Even though cutting up raw materials hastens their decomposition, you may not care about speed if you're building a long-term, passive pile. On the other hand, if your yard generates a profusion of waste and you want to produce compost as quickly as possible, some type of machinery may be a wise investment.

Buying equipment you use frequently, such as a mower, makes sense; you may want to rent other pieces of equipment. Make sure your local rental shop stocks the type of machine you want and that your vehicle is suitable for transporting it. Rental shops often provide a trailer for hauling large pieces of equipment. If the device you're renting has wheels, you'll need a smooth, gradual pathway to the composting area.

If you decide to buy rather than rent, do your homework first. Check with friends for their personal recommendations, and ask the supplier for a list of purchasers you can talk to. Compare models by reading articles in gardening magazines, and look up product evaluations in consumer publications. If you can arrange it, rent the machine you're thinking of buying at least once before making your purchase.

Mulching Mowers

Almost every major manufacturer of lawn mowers now offers one or more mulching models. (See Mulching Mowers on page 13.) Some are dedicated mulching mowers, and others convert from standard mowing to mulching. The single most important criterion to consider when shopping for a mulching mower is the horsepower (hp) rating. Since the blade must operate at high speed to cut and mulch efficiently, this type of mower needs at least a 4- to 5-hp engine. You'll find models ranging from 3 to 6 hp.

If you're shopping for a dedicated mulching mower, try looking for a model with a round, doughnut-shaped housing. That's usually an indication that you'll get a satisfactory mulching cut. Many dealers have lawn areas where you can test a mower before buying it. You want a model that doesn't clog, leave clumps of clippings on top of the lawn, or cut unevenly.

For the gardener who wants to mulch the lawn and, on occasion, collect clippings and shredded leaves for the compost pile, a convertible mulching mower is required. To convert a mulching mower to a conventional bagging mower, you change the mower blades, remove the discharge chute block, and add a bag. Find out if changing blades is convenient and how easy it is to attach and release the bag.

For either a dedicated mulching mower or a convertible model, a number of other considerations apply. How easy is starting the mower? How noisy is it? Is the handle adjustable and well placed for comfort and easy use? For safety

A mulching mower has a special cutter that chops grass blades into tiny pieces and deposits them on the lawn.

and to reduce vibration, is the handle covered with a thick foam or rubber cover? Is there convenient access for changing the oil? Can the cutting blade be easily removed for sharpening? Are the wheels metal, and do they have ball bearings? Does the emergency blade brake stop the blade without killing the engine?

Dedicated mulching mowers range in price from $220 to $520. Convertible mulching mowers cost between $250 and $650.

Leaf Shredders

Whole leaves are bulky and awkward to store. The garden equipment industry has addressed this problem by manufacturing shredders designed specifically for leaves. The two main types of leaf shredders are leaf blowers that can be reversed to suck in leaves and shred them with a knife, and dedicated leaf shredders with either a filament or a metal blade. Many people opt for a leaf blower because they can also use it to vacuum the leaves into a pile before shredding them.

Dedicated leaf shredders are electrically powered. You don't have to worry about fueling an electric machine, but you must deal with a power cord that may limit the areas in which you can operate the shredder. Leaf blowers are available in electric and gas-powered models. The gas-driven machines are much noisier and require frequent cleaning of the air filter.

Top: A reversible leaf blower allows you to vacuum leaves into a pile and then shred them.
Bottom: The smaller the pieces of woody waste, the faster they decompose. The amount of wood you typically collect should dictate whether you invest in a mechanical chipper-shredder or a manual system, such as pruners or a machete.

Ask for a demonstration of the leaf shredders you're evaluating. Observe how fast a machine works and how well it reduces material. Also compare the noise levels, and find out what safety features are built-in.

On a dedicated leaf shredder, the mouth of the hopper should be large and accessible, and the discharge should be where it's easy to collect the shredded leaves. Check to see whether leaves blow back out of the hopper. Most important, find out—not just from the dealer but also from customers who own the machine—how well the machine works with wet leaves. On a leaf blower, find out how well the blower works in reverse and whether it can suck up and shred wet leaves.

The price of a dedicated leaf shredder ranges from $100 to $285. Reversible leaf blowers with a shredding mechanism cost from $75 to $200.

A chipper-shredder chips branches in the side chute and shreds a variety of yard waste in the top chute. Use eye, ear, and hand protection when operating heavy equipment like this.

Chipper-Shredders

This type of equipment allows you to shred leaves and other garden waste in a large upright hopper and to chip branches in a side chute. Although you can buy a dedicated leaf shredder as the previous section discussed or a dedicated chipper, most home composters opt for a combination chipper-shredder so they can process more types of materials.

The purchase of a quality chipper-shredder involves a sizable investment—usually at least $500 and perhaps as much as $1,400. The first decision is whether your property generates enough waste each year to justify buying rather than occasionally renting. If purchasing makes sense for you, then shop carefully for a model that will fulfill your needs.

Chipper-shredders come with electric or gas-powered engines. The gas-driven models are up to six times faster than their electric counterparts, although electric models are quieter and vibrate less.

The two main types of cutting mechanisms are rigid knife-blades and swinging or fixed hammers. Most chipper-shredders have both mechanisms—blades for chipping and hammers for shredding. Look for a model with both types of cutters rather than just hammers. The blades allow you to process larger branches—as large as 3 inches in diameter with some models—to a single chip size. The hammers cut smaller material only—pieces up to 1¼ or 1½ inches in diameter with most models—but you can control the size of the chips by changing the screen on the discharge port. However, the screen can clog and cause the engine to stall more easily than when you're operating the chipping blades.

Key considerations in choosing a chipper-shredder are the power and quality of the engine, the diameter rating of the cutters, overall sturdiness, and maneuverability. Look for a model with a quality engine and the most power you can afford. Also get the largest diameter rating your budget allows. Inspect carefully for signs of solid construction. For example, the nuts and bolts should have lock washers instead of self-tapping screws. Make sure changing the oil on a gas-powered model is easy and that access to the discharge screen is convenient. If you plan to use the machine in a different place than you store it, be certain you can maneuver it easily.

Check for safety features. The machine should be designed to keep hands away from the cutting mechanisms. The instrument for pushing material into the hopper should also keep clear of the cutters. Find out whether the ends of the branches feed through the chute easily and whether material is typically thrown back out of either the hopper or the chute.

Don't buy a machine before finding out whether it can really process the size and type of branches you want it to. Some machines may only be able to handle the largest diameter mentioned in the literature if the branches are straight. The relative softness or hardness of the wood also affects the ability of the machine to process material. Take samples of the types and diameters of wood you'll be chipping to the dealer for a test run.

The price of a chipper-shredder for home use ranges from $300 to more than $1,400. Many quality models are available for between $500 and $600.

Machetes

Ambitious gardeners can use the shredder with a rich cultural history—the machete. Although it won't cut branches as finely as a mechanical shredder, a machete can be used to greatly reduce the volume of brush and small limbs for a slow, passive compost pile.

The secret to using a machete is to get one with a fair amount of weight in the tip of the blade and to use a rhythmic beat when working. Always cut away from your body, since machetes make deep, wicked wounds. An effective machete should cost no more than $30.

SELECTING COMPOSTING TOOLS AND SUPPLIES

The following are some of the composting tools and supplies available from garden centers and catalog companies. (See page 93 for a list of mail-order sources.)

Forks

All garden forks aren't alike: Some have three tines and others four or more. Each type has an appropriate role in the composting process. Loose, stringy materials—such as straw, alfalfa, or freshly cut weeds—are best handled with a three-tined fork, which is usually a lightweight pitchfork used for working with hay. The finer and less stringy the material,

Compost Machinery Safety Tips

Carefully heed all the instructions that come with a piece of machinery. Also be aware of these basic safety guidelines when you operate composting equipment.

• Always use cutting, shredding, or chipping tools with respect and caution and when fully alert.

• Wear a long-sleeved shirt and heavy work pants to protect your skin from flying debris.

• Wear a pair of antinoise ear mufflers or foam earplugs. Some chipper-shredders can produce enough noise to damage unprotected ears.

• Wear eye protection. Some products come with a pair of plastic safety goggles, although they sometimes fog over during the exertion of the job. Screen goggles, which are worn by professional loggers, are preferable since they stop all debris and don't fog over.

• For most tasks, a pair of sturdy, tight-fitting leather gloves will protect your hands and add a measure of comfort.

• Do not wear loose clothing that can get caught in the moving parts of the machinery.

• Keep your hands away from the mouth of the feeding hopper on a shredder and away from the discharge chute on a mower. Use a long stick to feed material into the hopper. If any material becomes clogged, turn off the machine, disconnect the spark plug or unplug the power cord, and only then should you free the clogged material.

• Watch out for material thrown from the hopper or discharge chute; make sure no bystanders are exposed to flying debris.

• Never run a gas-powered machine in an enclosed space, since carbon monoxide gas produced by combustion is poisonous.

The three forks, from right to left, are a D-handled, 10-tined pitchfork; a D-handled, 4-tined pitchfork; and a straight-handled, 4-tined garden fork. A pitchfork has lighter, slimmer tines than a garden fork and is a superior tool for scooping; a garden fork is handy for scooping and digging. A cultivator appears on the far left.

Inserting a compost-aerating tool deep into a pile and then pulling the tool out has the effect of stirring the materials slightly.

the more efficient a larger number of tines. A four-tined fork works well with whole leaves. It can be used like a shovel to scoop up finished compost or like a spade to dig into it. Four-tined forks are usually available as heavier, broad-tined garden forks and as lighter, slim-tined pitchforks. A 10-tined scoop fork is even easier to use with manure and compost than a shovel.

Make sure the fork has forged tines, not formed-wire tines. The lighter the fork, the easier it is to handle. A short, D-handled fork is handy if you don't have much maneuvering room, such as when you're turning compost in a multiple-bin system. Otherwise, for leverage and a healthy reach, get the longest handle suitable for your height. Select a hardwood handle without knots and with the straightest, most compact grain. The striping of the grain should run parallel all the way into the socket.

A quality garden fork costs from $40 to $70.

Compost-Aerating Tools

Many mail-order companies sell an aerating tool that you insert into a pile and then pull out, causing flanges at the bottom to open and fluff the compost. Although the tool works adequately, you probably won't need it if you build your pile properly. If the pile has collapsed into an anaerobic mess, it can be turned with a garden fork as easily as stirred with an aerating tool. Also, turning the pile allows you to investigate what went wrong and to add extra moisture if required.

A compost-aerating tool costs $15 to $20.

Compost Thermometers

A thermometer isn't really necessary to tell whether a pile is heating up, when to turn a pile, or to identify finished compost. Sticking your fist into a pile tells you if the pile is hot. A little experience will soon reveal the proper timing for turning a pile. And you'll soon be able to tell when compost is ready simply by looking at, smelling, and feeling the pile.

However, a thermometer is useful in indicating when the pile is hot enough to kill most weed seeds and disease organisms. Monitoring the thermometer can tell you whether the pile is becoming too hot, threatening the beneficial microorganisms. If too much heating occurs, the thermometer lets you know precisely when to turn the pile to cool it down.

Almost all compost thermometers are long-pronged devices with a temperature dial. Look for a stainless steel model with a metal probe at least 12 inches long. A compost thermometer should be able to register temperatures to at least 180° F. This type of thermometer costs between $14 and $40—the more expensive models are laboratory grade.

For about $75, you can buy a thermometer with a sensor that you place in the middle of the pile and a remote digital readout that you put indoors.

Compost Activators

Many mail-order companies and retail nurseries sell a wide range of compost activators, also known as inoculants, bioactivators, biocatalysts, and stimulators. These blends of aerobic bacteria, fungi, actinomycetes, and enzymes are supposed to speed up the composting process, help the pile achieve higher temperatures, and encourage thorough digestion of wastes.

Some home composters feel that activators are helpful, although many experts assert that they're unnecessary, since waste materials already contain the bacteria and other microorganisms needed for the composting process. In the words of one compost researcher, "Refuse carries the seeds of its own destruction." The microorganisms also abound in garden soil, so throwing a handful of soil on the compost pile will contribute even more microbes to the process than the refuse itself.

Compost activators are sold in granular and powder forms. The powder can be mixed with water and sprinkled on a pile. Enough activator to add to an average-sized pile costs between $3 and $15.

Pile Covers

Almost any compost system should be covered from time to time—for example, to keep out the rain or to prevent the pile from drying out too quickly during windy weather. Look for an impermeable cover that's flexible enough to conform to the shape of the pile. Most home composters opt for a tarp, choosing plastic since it's much less expensive than canvas. Get one made of an ultraviolet-protected PVC material that has been woven and stitched with reinforced seams. The cost depends on the size and quality of the tarp.

Wheelbarrows and Garden Carts

Transporting raw materials to the composting area requires either a large-capacity wheelbarrow or a good-sized garden cart. The largest wheelbarrows hold 6 cubic feet; the largest garden carts hold 18 cubic feet. A garden cart is a better choice for moving bulky materials, such as leaves, straw, or hay. A wheelbarrow is better for distributing finished compost to nooks and crannies in the garden.

If you want a wheelbarrow, get one with a pneumatic tire since it's easier to push. Sturdy,

Any kind of impermeable material found around the house can serve as a cover for a compost bin. Here, corrugated roofing makes a colorful cover.

This riddle, or small round sifter with wood sides, sifts compost effectively. A larger sifter that fits over a garden cart may be desirable for processing large quantities of compost.

rustproof polyethylene wheelbarrows are now available in addition to the standard metal type. A quality wheelbarrow costs between $45 and $90.

A garden cart big enough to move bulky organic matter usually has a bottom and sides made from weather-resistant plywood reinforced at the edges with metal. The higher-quality carts have zinc-coated steel edges, and the lower-quality carts are trimmed with a lighter-gauge galvanized steel. On both types the front panel lifts out for easy dumping. One type of metal-walled cart folds for easy storage, but its carrying capacity is only 11 cubic feet. The best models have large-diameter pneumatic tires and a ball-bearing axle. Carts with two separate legs may sink into the ground more readily when filled than models with a single metal-loop leg running the width of the cart. Be prepared to spend between $125 and $200 for a worthwhile garden cart.

Compost Sifters

Sometimes, you'll need to sieve finished compost to collect fine-textured material for potting mixes. You can either make a sifter or buy one.

A particularly useful sifter consists of a screen attached to a frame that you can set across the top of a wheelbarrow or garden cart. To make the sifter, nail 2 by 4s together to form a frame. Allow each board to protrude several inches on each side, so that you can use the ends as handles. Cover one side of the frame with 1/8- or 1/4-inch galvanized hardware cloth, and nail or screw strips of wood on top of the hardware cloth to hold it in place.

Buy a sifter if you don't want to make your own. The least expensive are metal sifters, which are usually round, and plastic sifters—they cost from $15 to $20. Riddles, or round sifters with wood sides, and rectangular sifters large enough to straddle a wheelbarrow or garden cart cost around $30.

Kitchen Compost Containers

Saving kitchen scraps in an old bucket or yogurt container often leads to an unsightly, smelly, fly-infested kitchen. The more pleasant and sanitary way to collect kitchen scraps is to acquire a wide-mouthed ceramic crock or a stainless-steel bucket with a well-seated lid.

Some retail nurseries and mail-order sources sell special compost buckets, although you may find a suitable bucket in a hardware store. You'll pay from $5 to $30 for a respectable compost bucket.

Another simple, effective solution is to retrofit a drawer just below the countertop to receive scraps. A stainless-steel food pan and lid used for steam tables or chafing dishes makes a good receptacle for scraps. The pans are usually 12 by 20 inches or 12 by 10 inches with a depth of 2½, 4, 6, or 8 inches. Restaurant-supply stores sell food pans for between $10 and $25 each.

To install the pan, remove the drawer and insert full-extension drawer slides near the top of the drawer space. Cut a piece of plywood to match the drawer width, then cut a hole to fit the lip of the pan. When it's time to take the kitchen scraps to the compost pile, simply pop the pan out of its slot.

Mail-Order Sources

If your garden-supply center doesn't carry the composting supplies you need, you may want to obtain them through a mail-order source. The following list includes firms that sell compost bins, chipper-shredders, and other products related to composting. Some charge a nominal fee for their catalogs.

Ashby House, Inc.
170 North Brandon Drive
Glendale Heights, IL 60139
708-529-0020
Compost tumblers, chipper-shredders

Compost and Recycling Systems
Box 265
Fox River Grove, IL 60021
800-848-3829
Compost bins, compost activators

Dalen Corp.
11110 Gilbert Drive
Knoxville, TN 37932
615-966-3256
Compost bins, compost aerating tools

Evergreen Bins
5301 Shilshole Avenue NW
Box 70307
Seattle, WA 98107
206-783-7095
Compost bins

Flowtron Outdoor Products
2 Main Street
Melrose, MA 02146
617-324-8400
Compost bins, leaf shredders, chipper-shredders, compost activators, compost aerating tools

Gardener's Eden
Box 7307
San Francisco, CA 94120
800-822-9600
Compost bins and tumblers, compost activators, aeration mats, folding wheelbarrows, kitchen compost buckets

Gardener's Supply Company
128 Intervale Road
Burlington, VT 05401
802-863-1700
Compost bins and tumblers, leaf shredders, chipper-shredders, compost activators, composting worms, aeration mats, compost aerating tools

Gardens Alive!
5100 Schenley
Lawrenceburg, IN 47025
Compost bins, compost activators

Garden Way, Inc. (Troy-Bilt)
102nd Street and Ninth Avenue
Troy, NY 12180
800-833-6990
Compost bins and tumblers, chipper-shredders

Kemp Company
160 Koser Road
Lititz, PA 17543
800-441-5367
Compost tumblers, chipper-shredders, compost activators

Kinsman Company
River Road
Point Pleasant, PA 18950
215-297-5613
Compost bins, chipper-shredders, compost aerating tools, garden forks

MacKissic Inc.
Box 111
Parker Ford, PA 19457
215-495-7181
Chipper-shredders

Mantis Manufacturing Co.
1458 County Line Road
Huntingdon Valley, PA 19006
800-366-6268
Chipper-shredders

The Natural Gardening Company
217 San Anselmo Avenue
San Anselmo, CA 94960
415-456-5060
Compost bins, leaf shredders, compost aerating tools, compost thermometers, folding garden carts, sifters

Necessary Trading Company
1 Nature's Way
New Castle, VA 24127
800-447-5354
Compost bins, compost activators, compost aerating tools, compost thermometers, composting worms

Nitron Industries
4605 Johnson Road
Johnson, AR 72741
800-835-0123
Compost activators

Ringer Corp.
9959 Valley View Road
Eden Prairie, MN 55344
800-654-1047
Compost bins, leaf shredders, chipper-shredders, compost activators, compost aerating tools, garden carts

Rodco Products Company, Inc.
Box 944
Columbus, NE 68601
800-323-2799
Compost thermometers

Smith & Hawken
25 Corte Madera Avenue
Mill Valley, CA 94961
415-383-2000
Compost bins, compost activators, composting worms, compost aerating tools, garden forks, kitchen compost buckets

Tornado Products, Inc.
N114 W18605 Clinton Drive
Germantown, WI 53022
414-251-4600
Chipper-shredders

INDEX

Note: Page numbers in bold-face type indicate principal references; page numbers in italic type refer to illustrations or photographs.

U.S. Measure and Metric Measure Conversion Chart

	Symbol	When you know:	Multiply by:	To find:			
		Formulas for Exact Measures			Rounded Measures for Quick Reference		
Mass (Weight)	oz	ounces	28.35	grams	1 oz		= 30 g
	lb	pounds	0.45	kilograms	4 oz		= 115 g
	g	grams	0.035	ounces	8 oz		= 225 g
	kg	kilograms	2.2	pounds	16 oz	= 1 lb	= 450 g
					32 oz	= 2 lb	= 900 g
					36 oz	= 2¼ lb	= 1000g (1 kg)
Volume	pt	pints	0.47	liters	1 c	= 8 oz	= 250 ml
	qt	quarts	0.95	liters	2 c (1 pt)	= 16 oz	= 500 ml
	gal	gallons	3.785	liters	4 c (1 qt)	= 32 oz	= 1 liter
	ml	milliliters	0.034	fluid ounces	4 qt (1 gal)	= 128 oz	= 3¾ liter
Length	in.	inches	2.54	centimeters	⅜ in.	= 1 cm	
	ft	feet	30.48	centimeters	1 in.	= 2.5 cm	
	yd	yards	0.9144	meters	2 in.	= 5 cm	
	mi	miles	1.609	kilometers	2½ in.	= 6.5 cm	
	km	kilometers	0.621	miles	12 in. (1 ft)	= 30 cm	
	m	meters	1.094	yards	1 yd	= 90 cm	
	cm	centimeters	0.39	inches	100 ft	= 30 m	
					1 mi	= 1.6 km	
Temperature	°F	Fahrenheit	⅝ (after subtracting 32)	Celsius	32° F	= 0° C	
	°C	Celsius	⅝ (then add 32)	Fahrenheit	212° F	= 100° C	
Area	in.²	square inches	6.452	square centimeters	1 in.²	= 6.5 cm²	
	ft²	square feet	929.0	square centimeters	1 ft²	= 930 cm²	
	yd²	square yards	8361.0	square centimeters	1 yd²	= 8360 cm²	
	a.	acres	0.4047	hectares	1 a.	= 4050 m²	